THE
ETHICAL
BUSINESS
BOOK

A PRACTICAL, NON-PREACHY GUIDE TO BUSINESS SUSTAINABILITY

SARAH DUNCAN

MADRID | MEXICO CITY | LONDON
BUENOS AIRES | BOGOTA | SHANGHAI

CONTENTS

FOR OTHER TITLES IN THE SERIES...

CONCISE ADVICE LAB

SMALL BOOKS: BIG IDEAS

CLEVER CONTENT, DYNAMIC IDEAS, PRACTICAL
SOLUTIONS AND ENGAGING VISUALS –
A CATALYST TO INSPIRE NEW WAYS OF THINKING
AND PROBLEM-SOLVING IN A COMPLEX WORLD

conciseadvicelab.com

HOW TO USE THIS BOOK

The book is a gateway to a fast-moving topic, which is why it has now been thoroughly updated with new material. It gets the reader started on all the important elements of ethical and sustainable business practice, but it is deliberately concise.

I have drawn on the insights of a number of excellent books and papers on the subject. Sources have been kept as brief as possible in the main text, but if you wish to pursue a particular area in more detail, there is an extensive Resources and Further Reading section at the back.

You can also visit: ethicalbusinessblog.com for book summaries, additional articles, and downloadable reports and exercise templates.

If you are a business owner or leader, this book will provide you with the tools to start making a difference. If you work for an organization that needs change, this book will give you the ammunition you need to lobby the decision makers and present a robust case for adopting a more ethical approach to the business.

> *"You can't go back and change the beginning, but you can start where you are and change the ending."*
>
> C S Lewis

INTRODUCTION

DOING THE RIGHT THING DOESN'T HAVE TO MEAN LOWER PROFITS

This is a complex and sometimes confusing subject area. Let's start with some definitions (from the Cambridge dictionary):

Ethical*: *relating to beliefs about what is morally right and wrong.*
Moral*: *relating to the standards of good or bad behaviour, fairness, honesty, etc. that each person believes in, rather than to laws.*
Sustainable*: *able to continue over a period of time.* In relation to the environment: *causing little or no damage to the environment and therefore able to continue for a long time.*

* For the full A-Z of Commonly Used Terms, see page 156.

This is The Ethical Business Book. The word 'ethical' is used as an overarching term that covers better all-round behaviour, in this context in a corporate sense. Much of the content promotes best practices, not legal requirements. But as governments start taking their responsibilities more seriously (see The Big Picture - Part 1.2), we are likely to see companies incentivized more for good behaviour and penalised for bad behaviour.

In recent years, the spotlight has been very much on environmental issues, driven by the climate crisis. The term 'sustainability' has been used more and more – which aligns the ability for the planet to survive with long-term business survival.

Now in 2021, as a result of Covid-19, we are hearing more of the societal side of the debate. The importance of not just saving the planet (after all the planet will go on long after us), but saving a world that is safe and equitable for all of us to continue to thrive on.

Whether you choose to use the word ethical or sustainable, the important point is that when you review your corporate actions you consider not only your impact on the planet, but also on society. This will be a recurring theme in the book.

When I embarked on this book back in 2019, one of my main objectives was to highlight to companies the need to make tangible change – not just approach the subject as a tick-box exercise or, worse, simply a PR opportunity.

What I have learned is that the challenge is greater than I had appreciated. It is not easy for companies to retrospectively refit their business in a perfectly ethical and sustainable way. But organizations can make significant strides in the right direction if they really want to, and genuinely buy in to the associated benefits.

We all have a responsibility for protecting the people around us, and our planet. Researching this book has affected my own behaviour (in business and at home). But I also know I have a long way to go.

So I hope you will join me in making the changes (big or small) that you can and collectively we can help make a difference.

Sarah Duncan
Westminster, 2021

> *"We cannot solve our problems with the same thinking we used when we created them."*
> Albert Einstein

Business practice has come a long way in recent times. The rise of social media has resulted in the demise of big companies simply pushing products at people (at least in the traditional sense). The power now lies more in the hands of consumers.

We look to our peers and influencers to guide our purchasing, not to the advertising copy.

False marketing claims are quickly exposed. And bad service is magnified by social sharing. Customers are demanding transparency, and exposure to behind the scenes of corporations. Companies are now required to tell their story or find their 'narrative'.

The importance to both customers and employees of being associated with higher ethical practices has never been greater and will continue to be a differentiator for decision-making.

So, simply put, acknowledging and responding to this market dynamic will protect your long-term profits.

IN THIS PART we will start by exploring the benefits of being more ethical, and then look at how a company can get started on a postive path to more mindul and sustainable business practices.

PART ONE

- HAPPY PEOPLE
- HEALTHY PLANET
- HIGHER PROFITS

BAD BUSINESS •
OUTDATED VALUES •
ONE-WAY MARKETING •

PROTECTING PROFITS

1. THE ONLY WAY IS ETHICS

It is now widely accepted that businesses have responsibilities beyond simply making profit. But there are many chief financial officers who would prefer to ignore the moral debate.

So it's important at the very start to make both the ethical *and* the financial point.

The case for adopting more ethical and sustainable business practices is a strong one, which includes driving long-term revenue, reducing costs, and managing risk.

Here are some compelling commercial reasons to support ethical change.

BETTER BUSINESS (CUSTOMERS, EMPLOYEES, PARTNERS)	With the rise in more conscious consumerism, ethically responsible companies are rewarded with extra, more satisfied and loyal customers. Perceived irresponsibility can drive customers away.
	Employees are also more attracted and committed to companies perceived as having a moral purpose.
	And good businesses tend to keep good company - seeking out like-minded partners.
REDUCED COSTS	Sustainable behaviour can reduce costs as it helps in saving energy, reducing waste and cutting out inefficiencies.
MANAGED RISK	Voluntarily committing to ethical business practices can, in turn, steal a march on future legislation.
IMPROVED MARKETING AND COMMUNICATION	Companies with authentic and compelling stories to tell gain greater trust and engagement with customers.

To what extent do the most senior people in your business agree with these principles?

2. THE BIG PICTURE

When looking at business ethics and sustainability, a good place to start is the 2030 Agenda for Sustainable Development, adopted by United Nations Member States in 2015. At its heart are the 17 Sustainable Development Goals (SDGs).

These 17 SDGs recognise that *"ending poverty and other deprivations must go hand-in-hand with strategies that improve health and education, reduce inequality, and spur economic growth – all while tackling climate change and working to preserve our oceans and forests."*

By reviewing the SDGs, companies can draw inspiration in terms of areas where their business can make a real difference.

GOAL 1:
NO POVERTY
End poverty in all its forms –
everywhere.

GOAL 2:
ZERO HUNGER
End hunger, achieve food security
and improved nutrition, and promote
sustainable agriculture.

GOAL 3:
GOOD HEALTH AND WELLBEING
Ensure healthy lives and promote
wellbeing for all, at all ages.

GOAL 4:
QUALITY EDUCATION
Ensure inclusive and equitable
quality education and promote
lifelong learning opportunities for all.

GOAL 5:
GENDER EQUALITY
Achieve gender equality and
empower all women and girls.

GOAL 6:
CLEAN WATER AND SANITATION
Ensure availability and sustainable management of water and sanitation for all.

GOAL 7:
AFFORDABLE AND CLEAN ENERGY
Ensure access to affordable, reliable, sustainable and modern energy for all.

GOAL 8:
DECENT WORK AND ECONOMIC GROWTH
Promote sustained, inclusive and sustainable economic growth, full and productive employment, and decent work for all.

GOAL 9:
INDUSTRY, INNOVATION AND INFRASTRUCTURE
Build resilient infrastructure, promote inclusive and sustainable industrialization, and foster innovation.

GOAL 10:
REDUCED INEQUALITIES
Reduce inequalities within and
among countries.

GOAL 11:
SUSTAINABLE CITIES
AND COMMUNITIES
Make cities and human settlements inclusive,
safe, resilient and sustainable.

GOAL 12:
RESPONSIBLE CONSUMPTION
AND PRODUCTION
Ensure sustainable consumption
and production patterns.

GOAL 13:
CLIMATE ACTION
Take urgent action to combat
climate change.

GOAL 14:
LIFE BELOW WATER
Conserve and sustainably use the oceans, seas and marine resources.

GOAL 15:
LIFE ON LAND
Protect, restore and promote sustainable use of terrestrial ecosystems, sustainably manage forests, combat desertification, and halt land degradation and biodiversity loss.

GOAL 16:
PEACE, JUSTICE AND STRONG INSTITUTIONS
Promote peaceful and inclusive societies for sustainable development and provide access to justice for all.

GOAL 17:
PARTNERSHIPS FOR THE GOALS
Strengthen the means of implementation, and revitalise global partnerships for sustainable development.

For more details on the Sustainable Development Goals visit:
www.un.org/sustainabledevelopment

If they feel a little overwhelming, check out the World Business
Council for Sustainable Development's Good Life Goals. These
outline personal actions that everyone around the world can take
to help support the SDGs, including a guide to how businesses
can make the goals relevant to employees and customers.

For more details on the Good Life Goals visit:
www.sdghub.com/goodlifegoals

3. CSR HAS MOVED ON

The way companies prioritize different levels of ethical behaviour depends on their overall strategy.

TRADITIONAL CSR

This is a long-standing approach to social responsibility. It considers Corporate Social Responsibility (CSR) as part of a strategy where a company generates its profits without too much consideration for wider societal expectations.

However, once the profit is generated, the company then distributes some of the value created to projects, activities and causes that are important to stakeholders. These activities will ultimately enhance the wider image of the company and bolster its brand identity. Ethical behaviour is therefore 'bolted on'.

NEW BUSINESS ETHICS

Modern ethical businesses promote responsible behaviour as an opportunity to generate profits while at the same time living up to expectations of society. Rather than unilaterally dishing out money, they work with stakeholders to understand their interests and expectations. Ethical and sustainable behaviour for these companies is integral, or 'built in' to their core business.

Traditional CSR is now regarded as the old way – making a profit and then doing something responsible with it. The new way builds ethical purpose into the company at the *beginning* of the financial year, not the end.

As Simon Sinek puts it in *The Infinite Game*, the old way is *'making money to do good'*, the new way is *'doing good making money'*.

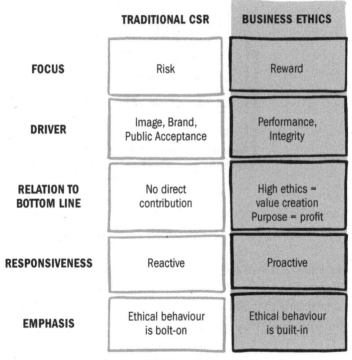

	TRADITIONAL CSR	BUSINESS ETHICS
FOCUS	Risk	Reward
DRIVER	Image, Brand, Public Acceptance	Performance, Integrity
RELATION TO BOTTOM LINE	No direct contribution	High ethics = value creation Purpose = profit
RESPONSIVENESS	Reactive	Proactive
EMPHASIS	Ethical behaviour is bolt-on	Ethical behaviour is built-in

Source: *Business Ethics* (Crane, Matten, Glozer, Spence)

4. IF YOU'RE GOING TO CHANGE, CHANGE FOR GOOD

Change for good represents a shift in thinking and practice across all business and involves a 'systems' as well as 'personal' transformation.

The book *Sustainable Business: A One Planet Approach* (Jeanrenaud, Jeanrenaud & Gosling) powerfully outlines the shifts needed for a company to work toward becoming a more ethical and sustainable business.

Area	Shift From:	To:
ADVERTISING	Creating consumer demand and fuelling consumerism.	Accountable and responsible advertising that discloses product origin, content, life span and disposal.
CAPITAL	Exclusive focus on financial and manufactured capital.	Focus that includes human, social and natural capital.
CONSUMPTION	A culture of individual hyper-consumerism.	Mindful consumption.
ENERGY	A reliance on fossil fuels and power supplies managed by big utilities companies.	Renewable energy resources.
GOVERNANCE	20th century models of shareholder capitalism.	New models of stakeholder capitalism.
INNOVATION	Centrally controlled, incremental, inward-looking innovation processes.	Building innovation ecosystems.

Area	Shift From:	To:
LABOUR	Labour merely as a factor of production in which work is exchanged for money.	Fostering entrepreneurship and encouraging creative and purposeful work.
LEADERSHIP	Individual 'heroic' leadership styles.	Leading through building commitment and engagement.
METRICS	The financial bottom line and quarterly reporting.	Measuring what matters and new metrics of success – such as the triple bottom line.
MINDSETS	Silos and ego.	Systems and eco.
NATURE	Conquering nature.	'Celebrating diversity' and 'learning from the natural world'.
OWNERSHIP	Shareholder models of ownership.	Different ownership models with alternative power and authority structures, pay scales and metrics of performance.
PLACE	Globalization of trade.	Building local living economies.

Area	Shift From:	To:
PRODUCTION	Sourcing the cheapest supplies possible.	Sustainable supply chain management.
PURPOSE	Exclusive focus on making profits for shareholders.	Achieving profits with a social purpose. The recognition that doing good and making money are not incompatible.
RELATIONSHIPS	Exclusive focus on competition.	Working in long-term alliances, and collaborating with investors, consumers and policymakers.
SELF	Focus on sustainability problems 'out there'.	Involving the personal and inner dimensions of social change 'in here' or change from the 'inside out'.
TECHNOLOGY	Mass production, stockpiling and global transportation of goods.	Decentralized production on demand at a local level.
VALUES	Top-down, competitive culture.	Caring, sharing, collaborating and serving the community. From 'me' to 'we'.

5. WHAT'S YOUR MORAL PURPOSE?

There is much talk about *purpose* in business these days, but what does it mean?

In short, your moral purpose should be greater than the products you make or the services you provide.

At the heart of establishing a wider moral purpose for your business is the recognition that doing good and making money are not incompatible.

Knowing what intrinsically motivates your people, what you're built to do better than anyone else, and where you can deploy that passion and talent to serve a need or solve a problem in the world is extremely powerful.

This matrix is from the book *Conscious Capitalism Field Guide* (Sisodia, Henry, Eckschmidt) and provides an excellent framework for establishing where your moral purpose is or should be.

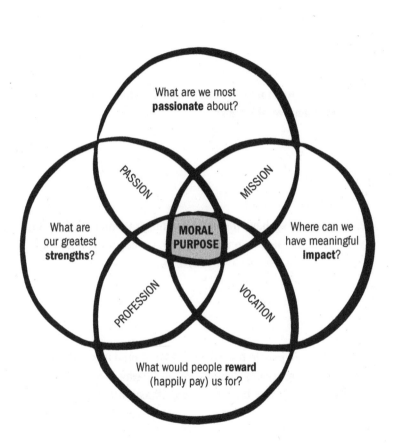

What are we most **passionate** about?

PASSION

MISSION

What are our greatest **strengths**?

MORAL PURPOSE

Where can we have meaningful **impact**?

PROFESSION

VOCATION

What would people **reward** (happily pay) us for?

1. **What is our business's greatest strength? What do we have the potential to be the best at in the world?**

2. **What are we most passionate about? What do we love the most about what we do?**

3. **Where can we have the most meaningful impact? Which big problems or needs in the world are we capable of solving?**

4. **What would people reward us for? What products and services would our customers happily pay for (maybe even a little more if we could deliver them in a more ethical fashion)?**

By answering these questions diligently and honestly, a company can get considerably closer to defining its moral purpose and working out what specific actions are needed to enact it.

Another good question to ask yourself is "*How do we want the world to change as a result of what we do?*".

Be sure to include employees. This will ensure future buy-in and guard against dilution, or fizzle out, as your purpose permeates through the business (see Part 2.9).

Also involve customers (and other relevant stakeholders). Find out what is important to them, and how this fits with your purpose-led strategy (see Part 3.4).

CAUTION:

If this is simply used to boost a brand image or to attain a short-term goal, then the impact will also be short-lived.

And remember, purpose without performance = PR.

6. THE TRIPLE BOTTOM LINE

The Triple Bottom Line = People, Planet *and* Profit.

This is a term first coined by sustainability thought leader John Elkington. It describes a business model that forces companies to focus not just on healthy profits, but also on high business integrity and environmental sensitivity – resulting in both successful business strategy and moral business practice.

Juggling the commercial and moral imperatives of people, the planet and profit needs time and thought to get right. It does, however, provide the company with a solid platform for future responsible business development and all the associated benefits.

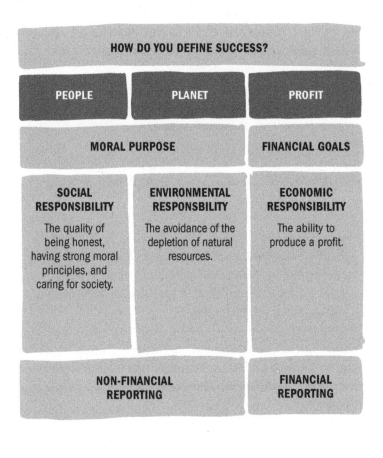

HOW DO YOU DEFINE SUCCESS?

PEOPLE	PLANET	PROFIT

MORAL PURPOSE		FINANCIAL GOALS

SOCIAL RESPONSIBILITY	ENVIRONMENTAL RESPONSBILITY	ECONOMIC RESPONSIBILITY
The quality of being honest, having strong moral principles, and caring for society.	The avoidance of the depletion of natural resources.	The ability to produce a profit.

NON-FINANCIAL REPORTING		FINANCIAL REPORTING

It should be noted that in his 2020 book *Green Swans,* John Elkington talks of retracting the concept of the Triple Bottom Line - not because it is bad, but because he is dismayed by how it is being used (or misused) in many businesses today.

He feels that many organizations are hiding behind the construct, just paying lip service and using it as a tick box exercise – without any real genuine desire to change the fundamentals of their commercially-driven business models.

Like so much surrounding business ethics and sustainability, it is important to embark on this with *genuine* commitment, not just for PR purposes.

And companies should avoid a 'race to the bottom', or being simply the least bad amongst peers.

Profit is not in itself a bad thing – businesses need to be commercially viable. In other words, it's hard to be green when you are in the red. It's how you make the profit and what you do with it that matters.

Start by developing ambitious individual statements of intent covering your financial goals *and* your plans to protect people and the planet.

INDIVIDUAL STATEMENTS OF INTENT

FINANCIAL GOALS

PROFIT

MORAL PURPOSE

PEOPLE

PLANET

7. SERVING SOCIETY AND PRESERVING THE PLANET

Financial reporting has internationally recognized frameworks. Non-financial reporting is less established and therefore less clearly and consistently measured. So as we await more internationally recognised standards for non-financial reporting, the question still remains: how can a business easily quantify its impact on society and the environment?

The Triple Bottom Line works because it incorporates people and the planet - up front. Where it falls down is when companies fail to attach tangible initiatives (with metrics and targets) to their beautifully crafted vision, value and purpose statements.

Not everything that counts can be counted, but you cannot manage what you don't measure - so it's important here that you set robust goals with clear accountability.

A good starting point is to re-imagine what business success looks like for your organization - establishing firm objectives and measurement criteria for Serving Society and Preserving the Planet. These need to sit equally in terms of importance alongside the monthly financial report.

SERVING SOCIETY

Can you give specific examples of how your product or service helps people?

What specifically do you do to 'serve' your employees, your suppliers, your neighbours or communities?

PRESERVING THE PLANET

Do you have a plan in place to reduce your environmental footprint (see Part 4.2)?

Where do you currently demonstrate product recycling, refurbishing, or remanufacturing (see Part 4.4)?

How do you encourage responsible consumption?

8. FIRMS OF ENDEARMENT

Many old habits and mindsets need to be challenged to become an endearing firm of the future.

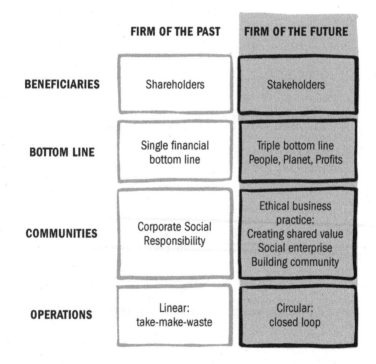

	FIRM OF THE PAST	FIRM OF THE FUTURE
BENEFICIARIES	Shareholders	Stakeholders
BOTTOM LINE	Single financial bottom line	Triple bottom line People, Planet, Profits
COMMUNITIES	Corporate Social Responsibility	Ethical business practice: Creating shared value Social enterprise Building community
OPERATIONS	Linear: take-make-waste	Circular: closed loop

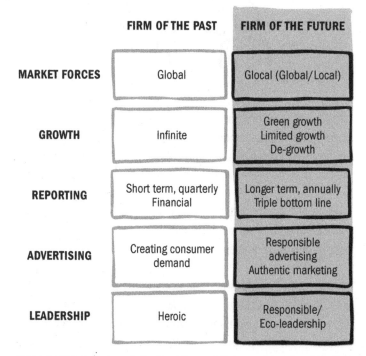

	FIRM OF THE PAST	**FIRM OF THE FUTURE**
MARKET FORCES	Global	Glocal (Global/Local)
GROWTH	Infinite	Green growth Limited growth De-growth
REPORTING	Short term, quarterly Financial	Longer term, annually Triple bottom line
ADVERTISING	Creating consumer demand	Responsible advertising Authentic marketing
LEADERSHIP	Heroic	Responsible/ Eco-leadership

Source: *Sustainable Business: A One Planet Approach* (Jeanrenaud, Jeanrenaud, Gosling)

9. FORGET THE A TEAM, BRING IN THE B TEAM

Many companies have a CSR policy that covers elements of charitable giving, community engagement and some degree of environmental sensitivity, but that fails to acknowledge or respond to the fact that the business as a whole does more harm than good.

If you really want to take your sustainability journey seriously, you should look at working with industry bodies, or towards appropriate accreditation.

Certified B Corporations are a movement of businesses that meet the highest standards of verified social and environmental performance, public transparency and legal accountability to balance profit and purpose.

If you decide to go for B Corp certification, you will join an ever-growing group of businesses that believe society's most challenging problems cannot be solved by government and nonprofits alone. By harnessing the power of business, B Corps use profits and growth as a means to a greater end: positive impact for their employees, communities and the environment. To view the process for your business, see assessment criteria and download guides and checklists, visit: bcorporation.net.

The Good Business Charter is a simpler accreditation which organizations in the UK can sign up to in recognition of responsible business practices. It measures behaviour over 10 components: real living wage, fairer hours and contracts, employee wellbeing, employee representation, diversity and inclusion, environmental responsibility, paying fair tax, commitment to customers, ethical sourcing, and prompt payment. For more details visit: goodbusinesscharter.com

There are other industry- or sector-specific bodies that can provide guidance, best practices and accreditation. For example, in the food service industry, there is the Sustainable Restaurant Association (thesra.org) that offers a comprehensive framework that covers sourcing, society and the environment.

For an overall understanding of ethical business practice by sector, subscribe to the magazine/website: *The Ethical Consumer* (ethicalconsumer.org). Here they rate businesses according to their 'ethiscore', which includes environmental, animal, people and political factors.

10. GOING UNDER THE ETHICAL SPOTLIGHT

So now we have raised some of the issues in relation to ethical business, here's an assessment tool to highlight your current areas of strength and weaknesses.

To complete this assessment online and receive bespoke feedback, visit: ethicalbusinessblog.com.

OVERALL COMPANY APPROACH   **Y/N/?**

My company stands for more than just shareholder value, and has a business model designed to benefit people, the planet AND profit (the triple bottom line).

My company has a clearly stated and understood *purpose* (beyond the products sold or services provided).

The board openly supports and prioritises sustainability and ethical behaviour.

Sustainability and ethical matters are fixed agenda items at board level meetings.

My company has a sustainability committee (or similar) made up of all levels of the business including senior management, OR a specific sustainability department.

ENVIRONMENTAL RESPONSIBILITY – Policy

My company tracks its energy and water usage, waste generation, and its environmental footprint.

My company uses a renewable energy provider.

My company has already achieved 'net zero' greenhouse gas (GHG) emissions.

If no, my company has a clear plan in place to reduce greenhouse gas emissions (and work towards net zero).

My company's environmental sustainability practices have been certified by an independent, third-party organization.

ENVIRONMENTAL RESPONSIBILITY – Culture

Environmental sustainability goals are clearly communicated throughout the organization.

Employees have received sustainability training.

Recycling is given priority and employees are trained on proper sorting procedures.

My company has responsible business travel policies in place.

Employees are incentivized to take public transport, or bike to work, rather than drive.

In the future, where possible, employees will be encouraged to work from home.

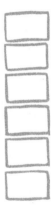

SUPPLY CHAIN AND PROCUREMENT

My company has clear supply chain policies in place to meet social and environmental sustainability criteria.

Environmentally preferable purchasing is set up for all office supplies, such as paper products and cleaning products.

Preference is given to suppliers who are local.

Social and environmental sustainability factors are given greater priority in procurement criteria than price.

SOCIAL RESPONSIBILITY – Community

Y/N/?

My company has specific community service policies and encourages employee volunteerism.

My company has a charitable giving policy and makes donations to non-profit organizations.

My company adopts the 'pay it forward' principle and donates a fixed amount of product or services for every paid purchase.

My company supports and/or sponsors local events and initiatives.

My company offers local apprenticeship programmes.

EMPLOYEES

Employees have been surveyed to establish their views and concerns around environmental and societal issues.

My company takes care of its people by paying a fair (living) wage and related benefits.

My company takes care of its people's mental health with a full employee wellness programme.

My company has in place a clear policy covering support for inclusion, equality, diversity and the elimination of any form of discrimination.

The following forms of diversity are represented throughout the company:

Race

Age

Sexual orientation

Religion

Gender

Disability

The following forms of diversity are represented at board level:

Race

Age

Sexual orientation

Religion

Gender

Disability

CUSTOMERS

Y/N/?

Customers have been surveyed to establish their views and concerns around environmental and societal issues.

My company's environmental and societal approach is clearly and transparently communicated to customers.

My company clearly communicates responsible care and use of its products to ensure maximum longevity and sustainability.

My company has customer initiatives in place to encourage product recycling.

MARKETING

Sustainability (environmental and social) plays a major part in the company's internal and external communications strategy.

All marketing claims are verified before being published to avoid greenwashing.

Marketing materials reflect diversity and include underrepresented and minority groups.

PROFITS RECAP

1. Start by reviewing the potential benefits to your business of becoming more ethical and sustainable
2. Look for inspiration from the Sustainable Development Goals (SDGs) and Good Life Goals
3. Consider your current CSR policies and how to become a truly ethical business
4. Look at all the aspects of the business that could change
5. Establish your company's moral purpose
6. Consider your ultimate goals in relation to your people, the planet and profits – the triple bottom line
7. Set initiatives to serve people and preserve the planet
8. Decide if you want to work toward accreditation and build this into your plan
9. Contrast the firm of the past with that of the future and draw up an action plan
10. Conduct an assessment to expose main areas of opportunity

"In looking for people to hire, you look for three qualities: integrity, intelligence and energy. And, if they don't have the first, the other two will kill you."

Warren Buffett

No business can be successful without good people. And good people gravitate toward good businesses.

By 2025, 75% of the workforce will be millennials – a group that will often refuse to work for companies if they are unconvinced of their ethical credentials.

As a result, companies with dubious or questionable ethical stances will fail to attract the top talent they require.

Other statistics show that highly motivated and engaged employees will:

- Generate 43% more revenue and 12% higher productivity
- Take five fewer sick days a year per team member
- Be 87% less likely to leave

Source: Engaging for success: enhancing performance through employee engagement (Macleod Report).

And as we shall see in this section, meaning and purpose play a major part in employee motivation and engagement.

IN THIS PART we will focus on how to develop your new ethical business approach to attract and retain great and diverse talent.

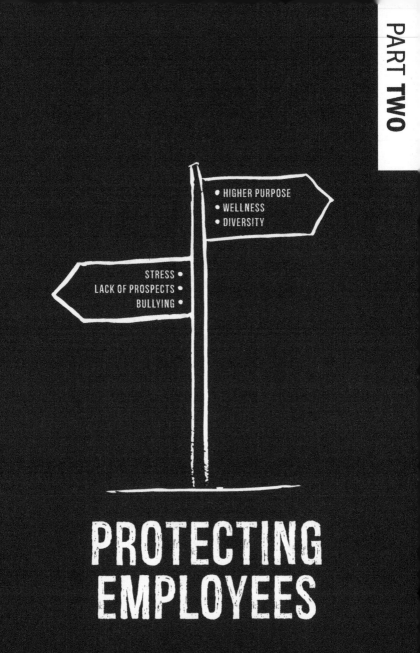

PART TWO

HIGHER PURPOSE
WELLNESS
DIVERSITY

STRESS
LACK OF PROSPECTS
BULLYING

PROTECTING EMPLOYEES

1. WHY SHOULD ANYONE WORK HERE?

Every company wants to attract the best talent, so start by asking yourself:

Why should anyone want to work for your organization?

Here are some great reminders of what makes a good company culture, from the book *Why Should Anyone Work Here?* (Goffee & Jones). A full staff survey example is also available at: ethicalbusinessblog.com.

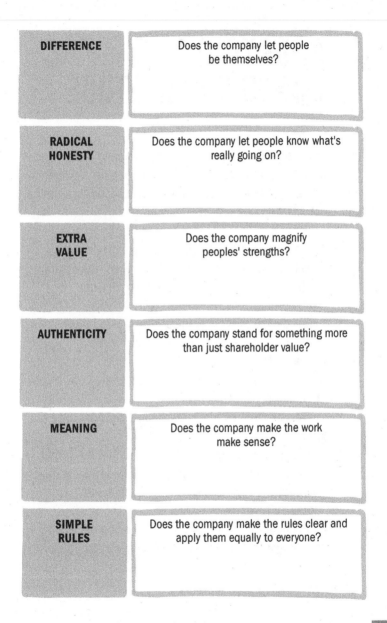

DIFFERENCE	Does the company let people be themselves?
RADICAL HONESTY	Does the company let people know what's really going on?
EXTRA VALUE	Does the company magnify peoples' strengths?
AUTHENTICITY	Does the company stand for something more than just shareholder value?
MEANING	Does the company make the work make sense?
SIMPLE RULES	Does the company make the rules clear and apply them equally to everyone?

2. ADOPTING A CONSCIOUS CULTURE

According to the book *Conscious Capitalism Field Guide* (Sisodia, Henry, Eckschmidt), when you walk into an organization, you can feel the difference between a 'conscious' business and a traditional one, and this is down to culture.

There are many books and approaches surrounding company culture. This book promotes the TACTILE approach – an acronym representing seven qualities for companies to consider.

- A high degree of **trust** permeates conscious businesses internally and externally with all stakeholders
- **Authenticity** is essential to build trust
- Feeling cared for and **caring** for others are core human needs
- Conscious cultures are **transparent**, because there's little to hide
- A strict adherence to truth-telling and fairness are at the heart of business **integrity**
- A continual desire to **learn** helps businesses successfully evolve
- Hire people with a strong fit to your company's culture and **empower** them to act intelligently and thoughtfully

Decisions and actions taken by employees shape the nature of a company, from the boardroom to the shop floor.

How 'Tactile' is your business?

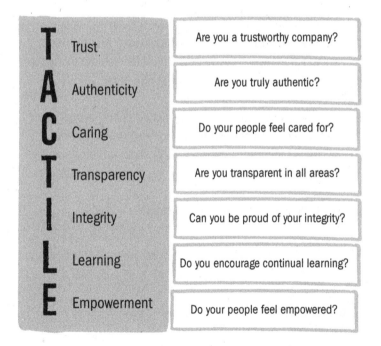

T Trust	Are you a trustworthy company?
A Authenticity	Are you truly authentic?
C Caring	Do your people feel cared for?
T Transparency	Are you transparent in all areas?
I Integrity	Can you be proud of your integrity?
L Learning	Do you encourage continual learning?
E Empowerment	Do your people feel empowered?

3. EMBRACE DIVERSITY

The best businesses benefit from a dynamic and diverse mix of people. Diversity and inclusion are now, quite rightly, hot topics in business. But while many companies are talking about it, there is still a very long way to go. And all-too-often we see signs of 'Divers(ish)' practices - businessess being selectively inclusive (depending on what suits the organization).

Like many of the big and important ethical business initiatives, this requires expert focus to enact properly and with full integrity. But a good starting point is to understand the breadth of the topic (and avoid being overly focused on just one area).

In her book, *Diversify*, June Sarpong highlights how our general fear of the 'other' (whatever 'other' is for you) subconsciously influences our behaviour. Whether we like it or not, 'other-izing' is something we all do, and 'other-isms' are something we all have.

The book looks at different types of 'others':

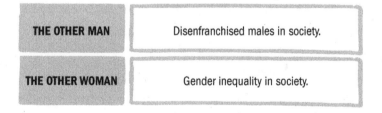

| THE OTHER MAN | Disenfranchised males in society. |
| THE OTHER WOMAN | Gender inequality in society. |

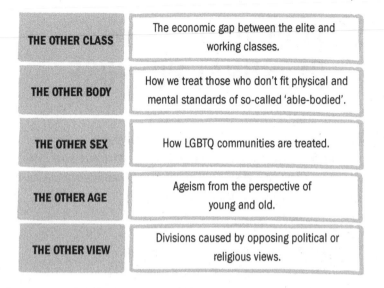

THE OTHER CLASS	The economic gap between the elite and working classes.
THE OTHER BODY	How we treat those who don't fit physical and mental standards of so-called 'able-bodied'.
THE OTHER SEX	How LGBTQ communities are treated.
THE OTHER AGE	Ageism from the perspective of young and old.
THE OTHER VIEW	Divisions caused by opposing political or religious views.

She proposes six degrees of integration:

Challenge your ism: beware of your conscious and unconscious bias.
Check your circle: don't just talk to the people you usually do.
Connect with the others: seek out people you wouldn't normally.
Change your mind: be prepared to accept another view.
Celebrate difference: find the best that alternative views can offer.
Champion the cause: there is more power in unity than division.

And try to avoid the cliché of male, pale and stale (or Yale) – an all-too-common scenario of male-orientated boardroom discussion and decision-making with no representation from minority groups.

4. FIND YOUR PERSONAL PURPOSE

Nothing gets done if no one can be bothered. And lack of moral purpose in business leads to reduced motivation. In his book *Drive*, Daniel Pink boils the essence of motivation down to three crucial elements, the third of which is Purpose.

1. **AUTONOMY** is the desire to direct our own lives.
   Example question: Are people allowed to get on with their work uninterrupted and be themselves?

2. **MASTERY** is the urge to get better and better at something that matters.
   Example question: Are people given sufficient training, support and tools to make them competent and confident in their work?

3. **PURPOSE** is the yearning to do what we do in the service of something larger than ourselves.
   Example question: Is the (moral) purpose of individuals aligned well with that of the team, department, or company?

Empowerment and training can cover the first two, but a strong company moral purpose, that is aligned with the views of employees, is required for the third.

If all three components are true, then high motivation levels will follow. Diligent, ethical companies will need metrics that measure whether all this is coming together for the overall good.

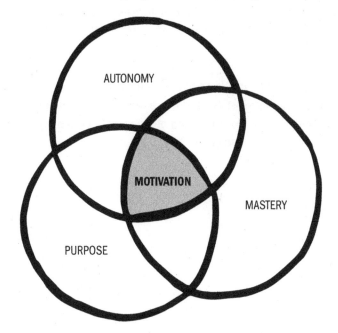

There can be various levels to such an exercise:
- Ask individuals to do it
- Ask teams to do it
- Ask the whole company to do it

Compare the results. Then identify and discuss inconsistencies.

5. IS YOUR TEAM DYSFUNCTIONAL?

Good businesses need functioning teams. There are five dysfunctions that can ruin the effectiveness and cohesion of any team, as outlined in the book *The Five Dysfunctions of a Team*, by Patrick Lencioni.

Each dysfunction builds on the previous, making it even more difficult to isolate just one issue in a team. The foundation, however, needs to be trust – one of the most important elements of ethical business practice.

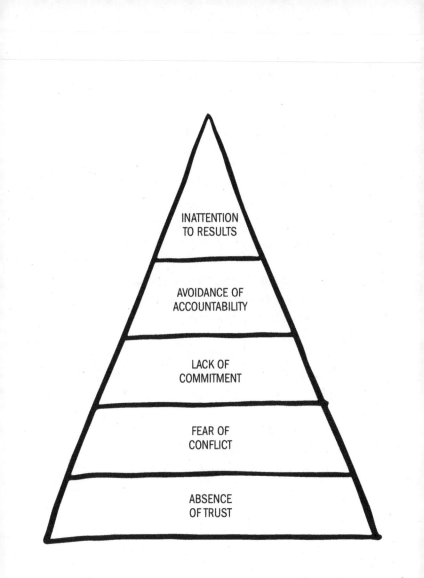

So, starting from the bottom (or foundation) of the pyramid and moving to the top, the important points are:

1. **ABSENCE OF TRUST.** Teams that are not open about mistakes and weaknesses make it impossible to build trust.

2. **FEAR OF CONFLICT.** Teams that lack trust are incapable of engaging in unfiltered debate. Instead, they resort to veiled discussions and guarded comments.

3. **LACK OF COMMITMENT.** Without having aired their opinions in open debate, team members rarely, if ever, buy in or commit to decisions.

4. **AVOIDANCE OF ACCOUNTABILITY.** Without committing to a clear plan of action, even the most focused people fail to call their peers to account.

5. **INATTENTION TO RESULTS.** Failure to hold one another accountable creates an environment where team members put their individual needs above the team.

So, in conclusion:

- Trust comes from overcoming invulnerability and admitting to weaknesses
- Constructive conflict needs to replace artificial harmony
- Creating commitment means removing ambiguity
- Accountability involves raising low standards
- Inattention to results can be addressed by removing status and ego issues

An assessment of this type has the capacity to expose uncomfortable deficiencies in teams, so think carefully about the implications and who should be involved before proceeding.

6. MAKE WAY FOR THE MAVERICKS

You need brilliant people to run a great business – particularly if you are to effectively juggle the needs of society, the planet and the bottom line. A handful of star performers can create disproportionate amounts of value for their organizations. These are exactly the types of employees looking to work for a company with a greater moral purpose, so attracting and retaining them is crucial.

But although the 'clever ones' can be brilliant, they can also be difficult. Their cleverness is central to their identity; their skills are not easily replicated; they know their worth; they ask difficult questions; they are organizationally savvy; they are not impressed by hierarchy; they expect instant success; they want to be connected to other clever people; and they won't thank you.

They also take pleasure in breaking the rules. They can be oversensitive about their projects and are never happy about the review process.

So traditional leadership approaches are often ineffective. Instead, bosses need to tell them what to do (not how to do it), earn their respect with expertise (not pull rank with a job title), and provide 'organized space' for their creativity.

There is also an almost endless need to restate the com[...]
moral purpose and verify that it aligns with what maveric[...]
being asked to do. Failure to do this will usually result in t[...]
pointing out the gap between strategy and execution.

Here are some dos and don'ts.

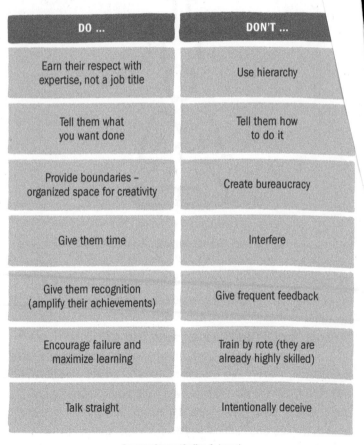

DO ...	DON'T ...
Earn their respect with expertise, not a job title	Use hierarchy
Tell them what you want done	Tell them how to do it
Provide boundaries – organized space for creativity	Create bureaucracy
Give them time	Interfere
Give them recognition (amplify their achievements)	Give frequent feedback
Encourage failure and maximize learning	Train by rote (they are already highly skilled)
Talk straight	Intentionally deceive

Source: *Clever* (Goffee & Jones)

7. FIND YOUR SOCIAL INTRAPRENEURSHIP

As introduced in the book *WEconomy* (Kielburger, Branson, Kielburger), purpose is not a singular task reserved for the higher-ups. Anyone can achieve purpose at work, and everyone should try, since it benefits an eager employee as much as it does the business.

The book promotes the idea that anyone in an organization can step up and volunteer to get involved or lead cause-related activities – like the company's community day, charity event or diversity programme. This in turn can get you noticed, even if it's simply bumping into senior executives to get budgets signed off. It's a chance to shine (and potentially push ethical causes from the bottom up).

These individuals are called Social Intrapreneurs – people within a large corporation who take direct initiative for innovations that address social or environmental challenges, while also creating commercial value for the company.

If you aspire to be such a person, build the following traits and reinvent your job with purpose:

A LEARNING MINDSET
Learn as much as possible as quickly as possible and see everything you do as an opportunity to learn. Remove the stigma from mistakes and errors; they are learning opportunities.

TRUST IN YOURSELF
Have a quiet confidence that you can take on whatever may come. Instead of fearing the unknown, develop trust that you can handle whatever challenge might be next.

HUMILITY
Be open to other opinions, admit your mistakes, spend time in self-reflection and recognize that you can't do everything yourself. Accept blame and share praise. Trust others instead of micromanaging.

AND
Be resilient, be tenacious and be creative.

8. THE AGE OF THE ECO-LEADERS

Leadership is always crucial when it comes to making great changes in business, and styles of leadership have evolved over the years.

The book *Sustainable Business: A One Planet Approach* (Jeanrenaud, Jeanrenaud, Gosling) outlines this evolution to what it calls the Eco-Leader (taken originally from Simon Western's writings of 2013).

The first diagram shows the evolution of leadership styles over the last century.

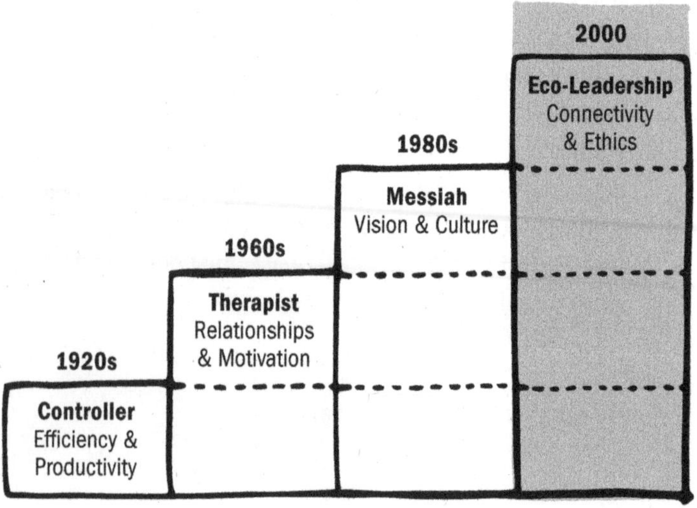

2000
Eco-Leadership
Connectivity & Ethics

1980s
Messiah
Vision & Culture

1960s
Therapist
Relationships & Motivation

1920s
Controller
Efficiency & Productivity

The book goes on to develop the thinking in greater detail, incorporating the four main styles and their interrelationship with ethical areas of business.

This is an interesting area to consider of oneself, or together as a leadership team.

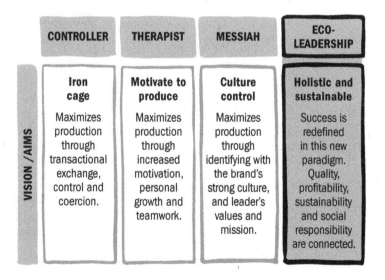

	CONTROLLER	THERAPIST	MESSIAH	ECO-LEADERSHIP
VISION / AIMS	**Iron cage** Maximizes production through transactional exchange, control and coercion.	**Motivate to produce** Maximizes production through increased motivation, personal growth and teamwork.	**Culture control** Maximizes production through identifying with the brand's strong culture, and leader's values and mission.	**Holistic and sustainable** Success is redefined in this new paradigm. Quality, profitability, sustainability and social responsibility are connected.

	CONTROLLER	THERAPIST	MESSIAH	ECO-LEADERSHIP
PERCEPTIONS OF EMPLOYEES	**Robots** Employees are seen as human assets.	**Clients** Employees are healed and made whole through reparation and creativity at work.	**Disciples** Employees follow the leader and aspire to be more like them.	**A Network** Employees are part of a network, with agency and with autonomy, yet also part of an interdependent, connected, greater whole.
LEADS WHAT?	**Body** Controller focuses on the body to maximize efficient production, via incentives and coercion.	**Psyche** Therapist focuses on the psyche to understand motivation, design job enrichment, and create space for self-actualizing behaviours.	**Soul** Messiah works with the soul. Followers align themselves to a vision, a cause greater than self (the company).	**Systems** Eco-leaders distribute leadership throughout the system. They make spaces for leadership to flourish.

	CONTROLLER	THERAPIST	MESSIAH	ECO-LEADERSHIP
ORGANIZATIONAL METAPHOR	**Machine** Takes a technical and rational view of the world, thinks in closed systems, tries to control internal environment to maximize efficiency.	**Human organism** Creates conditions for personal and team growth, linking this to organizational growth and success.	**Community** The Messiah leads a community. The emphasis is on strong cultures – the brand before the individual.	**Eco-system** Leads through connections and linking the network.
CONTROL	**Bureaucratic** Control via manipulation and strict policing.	**Humanistic** Control by emotional management and therapeutic governance.	**Culture** Policing is via self and peers. Open plan offices, lack of privacy and peer surveillance are techniques of control.	**Self-regulating systems** Control resides in the system itself. It requires resources and nurturing to self-regulate.

9. HOW TO AVOID A FIZZLE-OUT

Ethical commitment needs to run through the entire organization.

Without robust and effective internal communication, principles can easily weaken in the face of day-to-day reality, as this diagram adapted from the book *Brand Manners* (Pringle & Gordon) nicely illustrates. This is often described as a strategy/execution gap.

Board enthusiasm means little if initiatives are met with cynicism on the front line. Strategies need to be fully explained to be successfully embraced at all levels of the business.

Consider what initiatives you can undertake that will prevent high-level decisions from fizzling out further down the company.

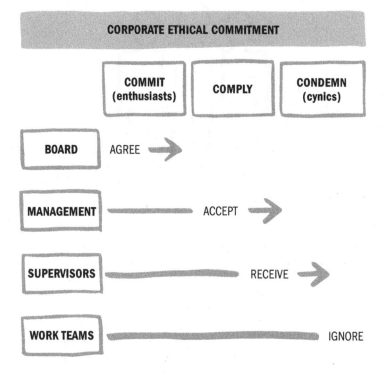

CORPORATE ETHICAL COMMITMENT

	COMMIT (enthusiasts)	COMPLY	CONDEMN (cynics)
BOARD	AGREE →		
MANAGEMENT		ACCEPT →	
SUPERVISORS			RECEIVE →
WORK TEAMS			IGNORE

10. SUSTAINABILITY IN ACTION – EMPLOYEES

Now that you have thoroughly thought through the importance of employees, use this framework to brainstorm ideas and initiatives for greater employee engagement and happiness.

Also, consider your communications plan. And weigh up the number of initiatives in relation to your resources – see Minimum Effort, Maximum Return (Part 5.9). Resolving to do a few things well within a short time frame may be the best approach.

Try not to generate these thoughts in an ivory tower populated by senior people. Invite all levels of employees to contribute to the plan.

INITIATIVES FOR GREATER ENGAGEMENT

REMUNERATION
e.g. Real living wage review

CULTURE
e.g. Creation of 'culture' team

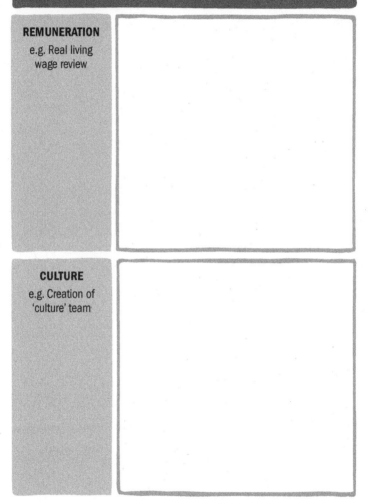

SUSTAINABILITY IN ACTION

INITIATIVES FOR GREATER ENGAGEMENT

DIVERSITY

e.g. Full diversity audit

WELLNESS

e.g. Staff food review; access to health and fitness club membership

INITIATIVES FOR GREATER ENGAGEMENT

COMMUNITY

e.g. Company-sponsored volunteering scheme

OTHER

EMPLOYEE RECAP

1. Ask yourself why anyone should work for your company
2. Consider a more conscious culture
3. Conduct an honest diversity audit
4. Define purpose and motivation within your company
5. Examine and improve any dysfunctional teams
6. Look carefully at the way mavericks are handled and managed
7. Identify and encourage any social intrapreneurs
8. Examine styles of eco-leadership
9. Anticipate initiatives fizzling out and put appropriate measures in place
10. Create an employee action plan

NOTES

> *"The toughest thing about the power of trust is that it's difficult to build and very easy to destroy. The essence of trust building is to emphasise the similarities between you and the customer."*
>
> Thomas J Watson

Being a trusted brand in the eyes of customers is surely the Holy Grail for any business. But trust needs to be earned.

Companies need to listen to their customers, understand what they want or need, and acknowledge them as human beings, not just consumers of product.

The ever-increasing numbers of conscious consumers are forcing companies to review their purpose – moving from selfish capitalism to responsible involvement in markets and society in general.

Businesses are nothing without customers – so ignore them at your peril and protect them well.

IN THIS PART we will turn our attention to customers and explore the importance of businesses adopting ethical stances to match consumers' concerns around environmental and ethical issues.

PART THREE

LOYALTY
TRUST
COMMUNITY

HARD SELL
THEM AND US
EXPLOITATION

PROTECTING CUSTOMERS

1. THOU SHALT LOOK AFTER CUSTOMERS

Let us start with a wonderful reminder of the importance of customers with the Ten Customer Commandments list. These can be traced back to Mahatma Gandhi, who reportedly taught them to his law clerks.

1. Customers are the most important people in our business.	**6.** Customers do us a favour when they call – we do not do them a favour by serving them.
2. Customers are not dependent on us – we are dependent on them.	**7.** Customers are part of our business – they are not outsiders.
3. Customers are not to argue or match wits with.	**8.** Customers deserve the most courteous and attentive treatment we can give them.
4. Customers bring us their needs – it is our job to fulfil those needs.	**9.** Customers are the individuals who make it possible to pay our wages.
5. Customers are not an interruption of work – they are the purpose of it.	**10.** Customers are the lifeblood of this and every other business.

Source: *The Sustainable Business* (Jonathan T Scott)

Consider the following:

How do these tenets tally with your company's attitude to customers?

Which elements can you take to design your own customer charter?

What ethical stances are particularly relevant to your category or product?

2. COULD CONSCIOUS CONSUMERISM BE KILLING YOUR BUSINESS?

Conscious (or mindful) consumerism focuses on helping to balance some of the negative impacts that consumerism has on the planet.

Responsible consumerism promotes eco-friendly ways of making products, as well as creating only the amount that's needed. Other factors such as pay equality and humane working practices also drive this type of consumption.

Conscious consumers want to use their individual actions to influence global impact. At best, they will simply avoid brands that are perceived as being unethical but at worst will actively boycott them (or 'buycott', as it is now referred to). This kind of conscious consumer action is actively promoted via some platforms that encourage the social sharing (and shaming) of unethical brand behaviour.

As conscious consumerism increases, those companies that fall short on ethical business criteria will lose more and more customers – ultimately killing the business if left unchecked.

So, to attract the attention of the ever-growing numbers of conscious consumers, your business needs to consider strategies that resonate with this group.

"Every pound spent is a vote for how we want to live."
Mary Portas

3. BUILDING RESENTMENT, ONE PURCHASE AT A TIME

There are still many who theoretically understand the shifting market dynamic to more conscious consumerism, but the sales figures aren't necessarily backing it up. At least, not yet anyway. On paper, and on the P&L, everything's still looking pretty healthy.

Without the personal drive of an enlightened chief executive or a collective board decision to change things because it's 'the right thing to do', ethical and sustainable initiatives can easily slip down the business agenda or get drowned out by other 'short-term' issues.

In these cases, companies may well be underestimating how many of their customers are starting to feel deeply 'compromised' by their current purchasing behaviour.

THE CONFLICTED CONSUMER

There is a growing customer type that appears to be extremely loyal – regularly purchasing products without, it would seem, any complaint. They like the quality, familiarity, price and convenience of a product, but are conflicted by other more ethically dubious elements of the brand – anything from single-use plastic packaging to tax avoidance. The lack of a better alternative, however, keeps them coming back. The question is, for how long?

As these customers' environmental and societal awareness increases, so will their resentment at feeling that they have no option other than to buy an ethically questionable product or service.

The very moment a competitor brand that matches the quality, price and convenience factors (but also shows a clear purpose and commitment to better, more sustainable business practices) comes into the market, switching will be easy.

And even without an easy alternative, the longer the resentment builds, the more likely they will be to change their purchasing behaviour anyway – not able to assuage their growing ethical conscience.

4. FEED YOUR CUSTOMERS' PASSIONS

If you are an owner manager who has started a business built around a personal passion or moral crusade, you have probably grown your customer base because they buy into and share your beliefs.

If, however, you are at the stage of reviewing what your company's moral purpose can or should be, you will need to think about what's important to your customers.

These questions will help you more closely examine what your customers care deeply about and how you can potentially make a difference in that area.

What ethical issues do our customers care deeply about?

* If you cannot answer this question plainly and with authority, it suggests that you may not know your customers well enough. If this is the case, you may need to pause and commission research to ask them.

If we could do something that would make a true difference in this area, what would it be?

* The key here is in the word 'true'. Do not complete this box with platitudes. You need robust, defendable claims.

What do we need to do to deliver this?

* For example: greater knowledge; budget; manpower; innovation?

Source: *Authentic Marketing* (Larry Weber)

5. WALK IN YOUR CUSTOMERS' SHOES

Let's look at customer needs in a little more detail. To fully understand your customers, you need to get into their mindsets – with a bit of profiling. This is a highly effective general marketing exercise, but for the purpose of this book, we will focus on ethical motivations and subsequent product development responses.

First, identify your different customer types (or target audiences) and then consider the following areas/questions – putting yourself in the place of the customer:

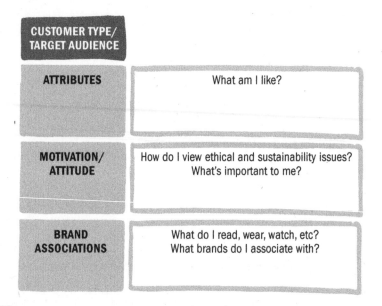

CUSTOMER TYPE/ TARGET AUDIENCE	
ATTRIBUTES	What am I like?
MOTIVATION/ ATTITUDE	How do I view ethical and sustainability issues? What's important to me?
BRAND ASSOCIATIONS	What do I read, wear, watch, etc? What brands do I associate with?

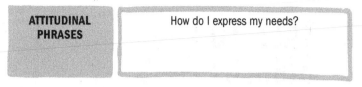

ATTITUDINAL PHRASES	How do I express my needs?

Repeat this exercise for all your major customer types and target audiences.

Now think again about your products and services. What bits are most important to each group? How are you different from the competition? What central messaging is appropriate? And where can you reach them?

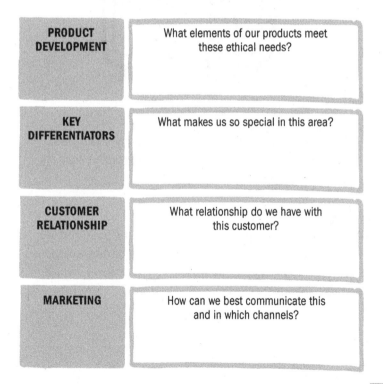

PRODUCT DEVELOPMENT	What elements of our products meet these ethical needs?
KEY DIFFERENTIATORS	What makes us so special in this area?
CUSTOMER RELATIONSHIP	What relationship do we have with this customer?
MARKETING	How can we best communicate this and in which channels?

6. TALK TO YOUR BIGGEST FANS

We often sit in boardrooms debating what our customers want and how they feel about us without actually taking the time to ask them.

As a business it's important to know where you are going wrong, but also what people love about you. Here are some questions to ask your most loyal customers (or your employees, supplier partners and other stakeholders).

What do you love most about this company or brand?

What does this company or brand do for you that no one else does?

If this company or brand ceased to exist, what would be lost? What would you miss the most?

Source: *Conscious Capitalism Field Guide* (Sisodia, Henry, Eckschmidt)

These need to be real answers from real customers. Do not answer them internally with fanciful or 'ideal' responses that make everyone feel good.

7. IS ANYONE REALLY LISTENING?

If we are taking the time to ask customers (and other stakeholders) for input and feedback on ethical matters, it's important that we listen properly – a highly underrated skill.

The most successful people in business listen more than they speak, so that they fully understand a situation. Note: the words *listen* and *silent* share the same letters.

How good are you at listening?

Get the members of your team to fill this out privately first so that their answers are honest. Then facilitate a session in which they discuss their listening deficiencies.

Improve listening for better working effectiveness – internally and externally. If there are external listening problems, then immediately revisit the 'Talk to Your Biggest Fans' exercise.

Y/N

Dreaming
I am often thinking about something else while the other person is talking.

Answer Preparing
During conversations, I am often waiting for a pause, so I can spit out an answer that I'm already preparing.

Compulsive/Impulsive
I often say something without thinking first or to fill a silence.

Ambushing
I often fake listen just so I can get in my comments.

Judging
I practise selective listening. I hear the things I want to hear based upon my own prejudices.

Not Fully Present
I'm often unaware of the message the person is sending through body language and/or vocal intonation.

Noise-Induced Stress
I often embark on a call or meeting when there is background noise in the environment to hinder my ability to listen.

Comparing
I listen through filters, based on past experiences with other customers/colleagues.

Source: *The Salesperson's Secret Code* (Mills, Ridley, Laker & Chapman)

8. TIME TO PAY IT FORWARD?

We are only as good as the good we do. If a company really wants to put their money where their mouth is, considering their *nonpaying* customers in the business model will achieve this.

This may well involve giving away products or services for free.

This approach is outlined in the book *Authentic Marketing* (Larry Weber). Weber recommends asking the following big questions:

Who in the world would most benefit if they had access to our products/services?

How can we set up a programme to provide access to our products/services to those people in need?

For specific examples of this, see BOGOF Reinvented – Buy One GIVE One Free (Part 5.6).

9. MAKE WAY FOR THE MATURING MILLENNIALS

The rise in conscious consumerism and the desire for organizations to stand for a greater moral purpose is very much being led by the younger generation. And this is an important factor for companies to acknowledge.

Businesses must avoid having the wrong people tackle these issues. Work groups must be representative of all relevant factions and, specifically, recognize the importance of millennials/GenZ.

AS CUSTOMERS	AS EMPLOYEES
68% of US millennials want to be known for making a positive difference in the world.	88% of millennials say their job is more fulfilling when they're provided with opportunities to make a positive impact on social and environmental issues.
81% of US millennials said a successful business needs to have a genuine purpose that resonates with people.	78% of US millennials want the values of their employer to match their own.
81% of millennials expect companies to declare their corporate citizenship publicly.	76% of millennials consider a company's social and environmental commitments when deciding where to work.
	75% of millennials would take a pay cut to work for a socially responsible company.
73% of US millennials are willing to pay extra for sustainable offerings.	64% of millennials won't take a job if a potential employer doesn't have strong CSR practices.
	75% of US millennials define success as doing work that has a positive impact on society.

Sources: *WEconomy* (Kielburger, Branson & Kielburger), *Huffington Post*, *Cone Comms CSR Study 2016*, *American Express*, *Forbes*

10. SUSTAINABILITY IN ACTION – CUSTOMERS

Now that you have thoroughly thought through the significance of your customers, use this framework to brainstorm ideas and initiatives for greater customer engagement and satisfaction.

At this point, also consider your other stakeholder groups. For example, your supplier network. What initiatives would help forge greater relationships with your suppliers?

INITIATIVES FOR GREATER ENGAGEMENT

CUSTOMER SATISFACTION

e.g. Customer 'thank you' programme

FEEDING PASSIONS

e.g. Regional focus groups (qualitative research); e-mail questionnaire (quantitative research)

SUSTAINABILITY IN ACTION

INITIATIVES FOR GREATER ENGAGEMENT

PAYING IT FORWARD e.g. New BOGOF initiative (see Part 5.6)	
SUPPLIER RELATIONS e.g. Supplier 'charter'	

COMMUNITY

e.g. Local community events calendar

OTHER

CUSTOMER RECAP

1. Consider the Ten Customer Commandments and draw up your own version
2. Look at the rise in conscious consumerism and identify specific trends in your market
3. Consider how conflicted consumers may be building resentment towards your brand
4. Identify the ethical issues your customers care about and then feed their passion
5. Walk in your customers' shoes by examining their views and matching your products and services to them
6. Identify your major fans and actually talk to them
7. Encourage active listening internally among your teams and externally with customers and stakeholders
8. Consider who in the world could benefit from your product and how you can potentially Pay it Forward
9. Examine and quantify the large market of maturing millennials to see what impact they have on your business
10. Create a customer action plan

NOTES

> *"Right now, we are facing a man-made disaster of global scale. Our greatest threat in thousands of years. Climate change. If we don't take action, the collapse of our civilizations and the extinction of much of the natural world is on the horizon."*
>
> David Attenborough

Being environmentally friendly used to be regarded as a nicety in business – somewhat fluffy, something to appease environmental pressure groups, and probably rather costly and inconvenient.

This is no longer the case. The evidence now shows that reducing negative impact on the planet is a vital prerequisite of running a successful business. Customers demand ethical practices, and they actively 'buycott' companies that do not demonstrate them.

The definition of sustainability is that something sustains. So in essence, companies that do not protect the planet's resources will not endure.

Transforming into a sustainable, environmentally conscious business can seem very daunting, but it is important to look at the simple steps that can be taken first. You'll never achieve everything at once.

Instead of being paralyzed by the sheer scale of the challenge, head toward the easiest paths. If every company could simply start making the changes they can, the planet would be in a much healthier place.

IN THIS PART we will take a more detailed look at the range of actions businesses can take to protect the planet's resources.

PART FOUR

- SUSTAINABILITY
- RECYCLING
- CONSERVATION

GREED •
OVER-CONSUMPTION •
THOUGHTLESSNESS •

PROTECTING
THE PLANET

1. THERE IS NO PLANET B

According to the Global Footprint Network (2018), humanity currently uses the equivalent of 1.7 planets to provide the resources necessary to produce goods and absorb waste. This means that it takes the Earth one year and six months to regenerate what is used in a year.

In 2009, Johan Rockstrom and a group of 28 internationally-renowned scientists identified a set of planetary boundaries – nine environmental parameters within which humanity can develop and thrive for generations to come, so long as they are not exceeded. These planetary boundaries are climate change, ocean acidification, chemical pollution, fertilizer use, freshwater withdrawals, land conversion, biodiversity loss, air pollution, and ozone layer depletion.

In an Oxfam discussion paper of 2012 called *A Safe and Just Space for Humanity*, Kate Raworth combined the concept of planetary boundaries with a complementary concept of social boundaries – food, health, education, income & work, peace & justice, political voice, social equity, gender equality, housing, energy, and water - bringing them into a single framework.

In this framework, the social foundation forms the inner circle and the environmental ceiling forms an outer boundary.

Between the two boundaries lies an area – shaped like a doughnut – which represents an *environmentally safe and socially just* space for humanity to thrive in. It is also the space in which sustainable economic development can take place – hence the term *doughnut economics*.

At the time of writing, we are overshooting the environmental ceiling in areas including biodiversity loss, climate change and fertilizer use. And seeing a shortfall in our social foundation in areas such as gender equality, political voice, peace & justice, and social equity.

So the reality is that we are currently far from living within this safe space. It will take a collective effort from governments, business and individuals to provide a stable future.

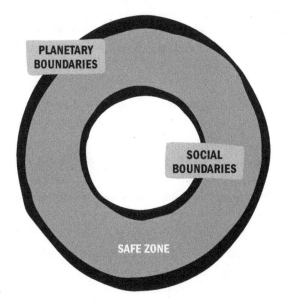

2. REDUCING YOUR ENVIRONMENTAL FOOTPRINT

This is a major priority for business in terms of tackling the climate crisis. It is a complex area and requires expert handling, but it's good to establish an understanding of some of the ambitions, initiatives and general terms surrounding the topic.

NET ZERO

An **environmental footprint** is the effect that a person, company, or activity has on the environment - for example, the amount of natural resources used and the amount of harmful greenhouse gases (GHGs) produced.

More specifically, a **carbon footprint** is the amount of carbon dioxide released into the atmosphere as a result of these activities.

> Every organization should be working towards a *zero* environmental (and carbon) footprint by conserving, restoring, and replacing the natural resources used in its operations.

Understanding your environmental footprint (including your supply chain) allows you to set in place clear actions and goals to reduce the negative impact, and achieve 'net zero'.

The GHG Protocol Corporate Standard classifies a company's GHG emissions into three 'scopes'.

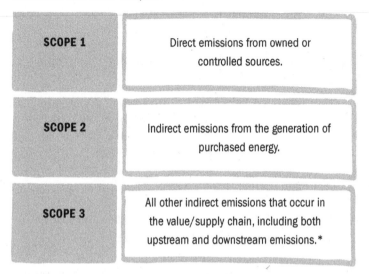

SCOPE 1	Direct emissions from owned or controlled sources.
SCOPE 2	Indirect emissions from the generation of purchased energy.
SCOPE 3	All other indirect emissions that occur in the value/supply chain, including both upstream and downstream emissions.*

*Upstream emissions = those that occur in the life cycle of a material/product *up to* the point of sale by the producer.
*Downstream emissions = those that occur in the life cycle of a material/product *after* the sale by the producer (including distribution and storage, use of the product and end-of-life).

1.5°C BUSINESS OPERATIONS

Scientists agree that we need to keep global warming to a maximum of 1.5°C to avoid high risk of catastrophic consequences for people and our living environment. To do so, it is generally accepted that the world needs to peak emissions by 2020 and halve them every decade until 2050.

The *1.5°C Business Playbook* is a clear guide to help businesses support this global ambition and includes four pillars that should be addressed in a company's climate strategy.

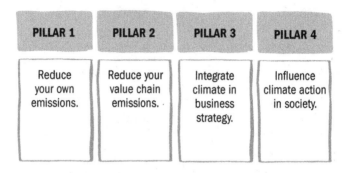

PILLAR 1	PILLAR 2	PILLAR 3	PILLAR 4
Reduce your own emissions.	Reduce your value chain emissions.	Integrate climate in business strategy.	Influence climate action in society.

The first pillar *focuses on a company's activities to reduce its own emissions, aligned with a 1.5°C pathway.*

The second pillar *focuses on a company's activities to reduce its value/supply chain emissions, with the same goal.*

The third pillar *addresses the alignment of the company's vision, strategy, value proposition, products and services. It means prioritising products and services that enable reduction and removal of customer and societal emissions, enabling resource-efficient lifestyles and consumption patterns.*

The fourth pillar *describes how to contribute to the 1.5°C ambition beyond your own business. This means, for example, influencing government policy and supporting industry initiatives.*

To download the full guide, visit: exponentialroadmap.org.

CARBON POSITIVE

The goal of net zero is great, but there are also companies working towards carbon positive operations.

Interface is an example of a company taking this further with their Climate Take Back mission. This invites industry to commit to running businesses in a way that is restorative to the planet, to use products and services to reverse the effects of global warming, and to create a climate fit for life. For more details, visit: *www.interface.com*.

CARBON OFFSETTING

Once you have reduced your carbon footprint, Carbon offsetting is a way of addressing residual carbon emissions (by purchasing carbon credits equivalent to your outstanding negative carbon impact).

Basically, it is a way of compensating for the damage caused by ones own emissions by supporting schemes designed to make equivalent reductions of carbon dioxide in the atmosphere. A simple example would be an activity such as planting trees.

By implementing *net zero*, *1.5°C*, or *carbon positive*-aligned strategies, companies will help support the UN's Sustainable Development Goals (SDGs) - see Part 1.2 The Big Picture.

3. NOT ALL WASTE IS BORN EQUAL

The headlines here are:
1. REDUCE the amount you use
2. REUSE product or product elements, wherever possible
3. RECYCLE what is left, wherever possible

The Waste Hierarchy model sets out the levels of options for managing waste in an environmentally helpful way.

It gives top priority to preventing waste in the first place. When waste is created, it gives priority to preparing it for reuse, then recycling, then recovery, and last of all disposal (e.g. landfill) – which should be avoided whenever possible.

STAGES	INCLUDE
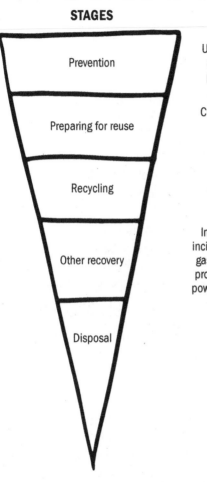 Prevention	Using less material in design and manufacture. Keeping products for longer. Reuse.
Preparing for reuse	Checking, cleaning, repairing, refurbishing, whole items or spare parts.
Recycling	Turning waste into a new substance or product (including composting).
Other recovery	Includes anaerobic digestion, incineration with energy recovery, gasification and pyrolysis which produce energy (fuels, heat and power) and materials from waste.
Disposal	Landfill and incineration without energy recovery.

Source: *Defra.gov.uk – the official website for the Department for Environment, Food and Rural Affairs*

4. THE CIRCULAR ECONOMY

The circular economy model is inspired by natural living systems, and promotes the fact that there is 'no such thing as waste in nature'.

Unlike the traditional linear approach of take-make-use-waste, a circular economy is a sustainable 'closed loop' model.

It creates value through product recapture and then recycling, restoring and reusing product elements in remanufacturing - thereby radically limiting the extraction of raw materials at the beginning, and the production of waste at the end, of a product's life. In essence, keeping products and materials in use for as long as possible.

ACCESS VS OWNERSHIP

The circular economy concept also challenges the necessity of owning products in the way that we are traditionally used to. It is access to the service a product provides that is important, rather than the product itself. Understanding this shift in mindset lays the groundwork to many of the practicalities of shifting our economy from linear to circular, and can be seen in many examples now from car sharing clubs to fashion rental.

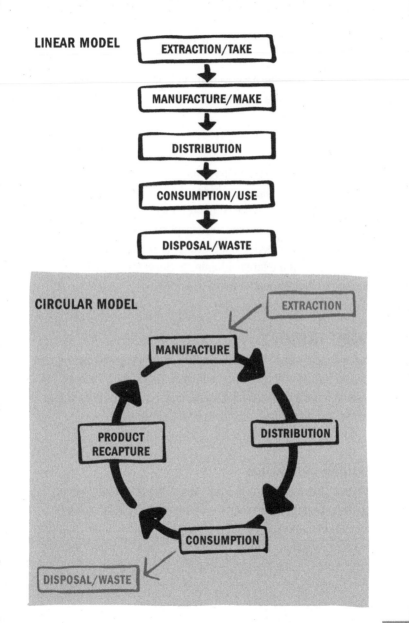

The circular economy concept has deep-rooted origins and cannot be traced back to one single date or author. Its practical applications, however, have gained momentum since the late 1970s, and there are a number of interconnected concepts.

BIOMIMICRY

Bio means life; mimicry means imitate. So biomimicry is the practice of imitating life – emulating the models, systems, and elements of nature to solve complex human problems. Examples include Velcro, whose inventor was inspired by the tiny hooks on burdock burrs (seeds) that stuck to his dog's fur, and the aerodynamics of the famous Japanese Bullet train, which was inspired by the shape of a bird's beak.

CRADLE TO CRADLE

This is a sustainable business strategy that mimics the regenerative cycle of nature in which waste is reused. Building on the cradle to grave approach of decreasing waste, cradle to cradle goes a step further and attempts to eliminate waste altogether.

NATURAL CAPITALISM

This is a global economy in which business and environmental interests overlap, recognizing the interdependencies that exist between the production and use of human-made capital (industry) and flows of natural capital (the world's stocks of natural assets).

THE INERTIA PRINCIPLE

This is a guiding principle of the circular economy, as introduced by Walter Stahel. *"Do not repair what is not broken, do not remanufacture something that can be repaired, do not recycle a product that can be remanufactured. Replace or treat only the smallest possible part in order to maintain the existing economic value"*.

Like many sections of this book, this is just a snapshot of what is a complex subject area. However, looking into how your business can adopt a more circular approach will undoubtedly contribute to longer-term sustainability.

For a great understanding of the opportunities around the circular economy, visit: ellenmacarthurfoundation.org.

5. CONSERVING ENERGY

The first step here is straightforward – switch to a renewable energy supplier.

But there are many other ways you can reduce how much energy you use and lower costs in the workplace.

SMART METERING

Installing smart meters can have the greatest overall effect on managing energy in the workplace and at home. Smart meters come with a display screen that shows the user exactly how much energy they're using and what it costs, in near real time.

TIME-OF-USE TARIFFS

Time-of-use tariffs are designed to incentivize customers to use more electricity at off-peak times in order to balance demand. These tariffs charge cheaper rates at certain times of the night or day, when demand is at its lowest, and higher rates at popular times. Shifting demand to off-peak times means relying less on polluting sources of electricity.

TRAVEL

Travel is another important factor. Can meeting technology reduce the need for physical business travel? If travel is essential, should a company commit to a carbon-offsetting programme? Are employees encouraged to cycle to work, use public transport or work from home whenever possible?

GENERAL

A good source for recommendations, downloadable guides and case histories to help businesses reduce their environmental impact is *CarbonTrust.com*. Their suggestions include:

- **SWITCH OFF**
  Switch off all non-essential lighting out of business hours.

- **LED FITTINGS**
  Replace traditional tungsten lamps with energy-efficient LED fittings to improve efficiency and reduce operating costs.

- **THERMOSTATS**
  Ensure thermostats are set correctly – increase temperature set-points for cooling and reduce set-points for heating.

- **TURN OFF**
  Turn off unnecessary equipment during the day and especially after hours to reduce heat build-up and unnecessary electrical costs.

- **INSULATION**
  Check insulation levels and increase wherever practical to reduce heating requirements.

- **MONITOR**
  Walk around your office at different times of the day/different seasons to see how and when heaters and coolers are working.

Positive change does not happen if this sits somewhere on a policy sheet. Intentions need to be converted into clear, specific action points for individuals to carry out.

6. CONSERVING WATER

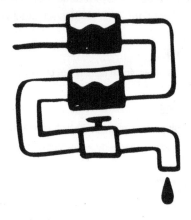

Each person, on average, uses 150 litres of water per day. If everyone in the UK adopted more water-saving habits, this could easily be reduced to 100 litres per day.

Businesses can play a big part. Here are some tips:

- **LOOK OUT FOR WATER LEAKS**
  We lose three billion litres of water a day in England and Wales due to water leaks.

- **INSTALL DUAL-FLUSH TOILETS**
  Toilets represent over 30% of water usage in the workplace. If your building is open to the public, this can be even more substantial. Dual flush toilets use six litres on full flush, which is less than half of a traditional toilet.

- **INSTALL EFFICIENT TAPS**
  Make sure all your hand basin taps are on auto shut-off.
  Also, you can buy aerators – these spread the stream of
  water coming out of your tap into tiny droplets. This will
  prevent splashing and save water.

- **FILL THE DISHWASHER**
  Always wash a full load of dishes to gain maximum
  water efficiency. If possible, change to a water-efficient
  dishwasher, as it uses the minimal amount of water
  necessary to clean and rinse.

- **ENCOURAGE SHORT SHOWERS**
  If your workplace has showers, spread the word that
  spending over five minutes in a Power Shower can use
  more water than taking a bath.

- **DON'T WASTE DRINKING WATER**
  The Department of Health recommends that we drink
  at least one litre of water each day (about six glasses).
  Many people waste water by letting the tap run cold
  before filling up their glass. So keep jugs of water in the
  fridge or install a water fountain that serves ice-cold
  drinking water straight away.

7. GREENING YOUR SUPPLY CHAIN

We've covered the importance of scrutinising your supply chain to reduce your environmental footprint, but embedding this into the culture of a business can be a challenge.

Here are some basic questions that can be asked throughout the procurement processes of any organzation (or indeed our own personal puchasing).

PRODUCTS

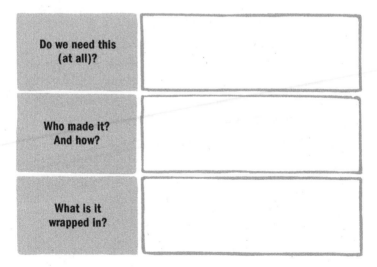

Do we need this (at all)?	
Who made it? And how?	
What is it wrapped in?	

How will it be transported?	
How will it perform throughout its life?	
What does it say to our customers?	
What is it made of?	
Where will it end up?	

Source: *WEconomy* (Kielburger, Branson, Kielburger)

NOTE ON PACKAGING

Packaging comes in many shapes and sizes: boxes, bags, cans, foam pellets, shrink wrap, tubes, paper, etc. – all designed to protect a product and keep it pristine or fresh. When considering packaging in your supply chain, make sure you cover the various types:

- **Primary packaging**: the wrapping or container handled by customers
- **Secondary packaging**: larger cases, boxes or bags used to group goods together for distribution, ease of carrying or displaying in shops
- **Transit packaging**: pallets, boards, plastic wrap and containers used to collate products into larger loads for shipping

SERVICES

Supply chains also include service providers. These should also be added to your assessment.

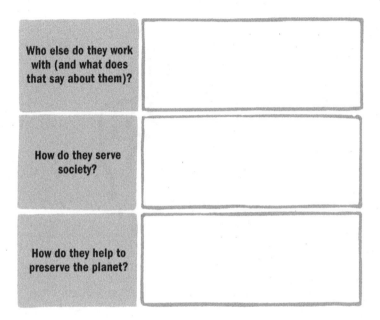

Who else do they work with (and what does that say about them)?	
How do they serve society?	
How do they help to preserve the planet?	

And a final note on the UK Modern Slavery Act, which came into effect in 2015. This requires companies to make a public statement on whether they have processes in place to look into modern slavery anywhere in their operations or their supply chain. Technically only multimillion-pound turnover companies need to publish a statement on this (on the main page of their website), but it's an area that all companies should consider.

8. ARE YOU AN ECO- OR EGO-WARRIOR?

Are you an Eco-Warrior – genuinely concerned with the planet and civilization as a whole? Or are you an Ego-Warrior – more focused on how your actions are viewed by your peers?

While clearly the latter has a degree of cynicism attached, the truth is that as long as you are adapting your behaviour to help protect the planet, the result is still positive.

The same can be said of business. Notwithstanding the importance of marketing authenticity (covered in Part 5), the motivation to create a more ethical and sustainable business can vary. For example:

- Some will be driven by a personal eco crusade
- For others, the positive PR will be an attractive factor (and fuel the corporate ego)
- Arguing the positive effect on the bottom line will delight the finance department
- HR will be keen to capitalize on attracting and retaining better talent
- Customer service will welcome a happy, committed customer base

Your customers will also have different motivations and reasons for selecting more ethical and sustainable products. For some it will be a genuine commitment to saving the planet. For others it will be a trade-off to feel better about consumption in other areas. Ultimately, the planet doesn't care what your motive is, so long as you do the right thing.

So the moral here is that whatever pushes the ethical agenda along in your business is positive progress.

9. OVERCOMING THE RESISTORS

There will always be some resistance to adopting ethical and sustainable practices. Here are some of the common ones.

Consider the issues and think of ways to overcome them.

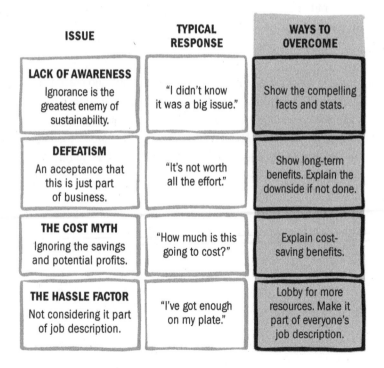

ISSUE	TYPICAL RESPONSE	WAYS TO OVERCOME
LACK OF AWARENESS Ignorance is the greatest enemy of sustainability.	"I didn't know it was a big issue."	Show the compelling facts and stats.
DEFEATISM An acceptance that this is just part of business.	"It's not worth all the effort."	Show long-term benefits. Explain the downside if not done.
THE COST MYTH Ignoring the savings and potential profits.	"How much is this going to cost?"	Explain cost-saving benefits.
THE HASSLE FACTOR Not considering it part of job description.	"I've got enough on my plate."	Lobby for more resources. Make it part of everyone's job description.

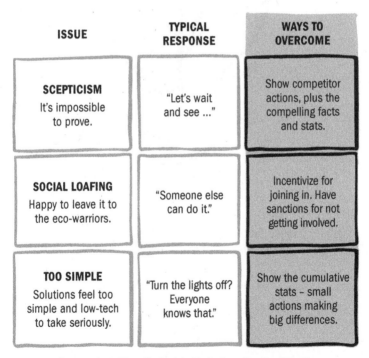

ISSUE	TYPICAL RESPONSE	WAYS TO OVERCOME
SCEPTICISM It's impossible to prove.	"Let's wait and see …"	Show competitor actions, plus the compelling facts and stats.
SOCIAL LOAFING Happy to leave it to the eco-warriors.	"Someone else can do it."	Incentivize for joining in. Have sanctions for not getting involved.
TOO SIMPLE Solutions feel too simple and low-tech to take seriously.	"Turn the lights off? Everyone knows that."	Show the cumulative stats – small actions making big differences.

Source: adapted from *The Sustainable Business* (Jonathan T Scott)

10. SUSTAINABILITY IN ACTION – PLANET

Now that you have considered all the ways you and your company can help protect the planet, use the following framework to brainstorm specific ideas and initiatives.

INITIATIVES FOR ENVIRONMENTAL SUSTAINABILITY

REDUCING ENVIRONMENTAL FOOTPRINT

e.g. Understand your current emissions and create a plan to achieve net zero

INITIATIVES FOR ENVIRONMENTAL SUSTAINABILITY

CONSERVING RESOURCES

e.g. Switch to renewable energy supplier; create an internal 'Green Team'

MANAGING WASTE

e.g. Create Reduce, Reuse, Recycle programme; conduct single-use plastics review

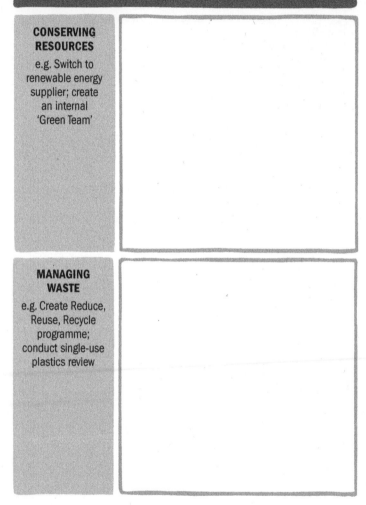

GREENING YOUR SUPPLY CHAIN/ CIRCULAR ECONOMY

e.g. Consider where linear processes can be replaced with a circular approach

PLANET RECAP

1. Work out whether you are taking more from the planet than you are putting back
2. Identify areas where you can reduce your environmental footprint (and achieve net zero)
3. Create a waste management plan
4. Consider whether you can move the business from a linear model to a circular model
5. Create an energy conservation plan
6. Create a water conservation plan
7. Create internal processes to green your supply chain
8. Contrast ego- with eco-warriors and harness their joint power
9. Anticipate areas of resistance to progressing as an ethical and sustainable business and develop plans to overcome them
10. Now create a full planet action plan

NOTES

"People who say it cannot be done should not interrupt those who are doing it."

George Bernard Shaw

Assuming a company is indeed behaving ethically, its marketing will immediately gain extra credence and authenticity.

Rather than scrabbling around for the standard calendar-based marketing clichés (Valentine's, Easter, Halloween, Christmas, etc.), businesses can instead focus on the genuinely interesting initiatives they are enacting.

In short, the marketing efforts of an ethical business are essentially self-defining, unforced and, therefore, genuinely engaging.

But don't be afraid of the halfway house – all businesses are a work in progress. Companies just need to be able to legitimately say that initiatives have been set in train and that this is part of an ethical journey to better things. Just be sure that any claims do not fall into the category of greenwashing. You will be exposed for false marketing, and this can do far more harm than good.

Stick to the truth, be honest and update stakeholders regularly on your progress.

IN THIS PART we will further explore the benefits and pitfalls of placing ethical beliefs and activities at the heart of your marketing and communications strategy.

PART FIVE

- ENGAGING
- AUTHENTIC
- HUMAN

GREENWASHING ●
DISINGENUOUS ●
MISLEADING ●

ETHICAL
MARKETING

1. MARKETING: FROM MANIPULATION TO AUTHENTICITY

Marketing has come a long way. Here's a nice reminder of its evolution and thoughts on the new age of authentic marketing practices.

The moral of this evolution is that modern companies must pay attention to their customers and evolve. Failure to do so will severely jeopardize customer trust – a crucial element in marketing today.

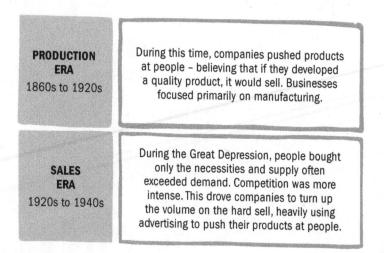

PRODUCTION ERA 1860s to 1920s	During this time, companies pushed products at people – believing that if they developed a quality product, it would sell. Businesses focused primarily on manufacturing.
SALES ERA 1920s to 1940s	During the Great Depression, people bought only the necessities and supply often exceeded demand. Competition was more intense. This drove companies to turn up the volume on the hard sell, heavily using advertising to push their products at people.

MARKETING ERA Mid-20th century	Here came a fundamental shift in focus: from the needs of the seller to the needs of the buyer. Broadcast advertising emerged, giving companies new ways to capture attention – to interrupt and manipulate. However, it was now done creatively – with likeable characters, celebrity endorsements, etc.
RELATIONSHIP MARKETING ERA Mid-1990s to early 2000s	Recognizing that acquiring new customers was more expensive than keeping current ones, marketing folk began to value the role of relationships and brand loyalty. Big data emerged as a means to help companies better understand audience segmentation. Direct marketing became a staple tactic.
DIGITAL ENGAGEMENT ERA 2000s	As the internet and digital/social media started to become engrained in our culture, a seismic shift happened. A massive power shift put the reins directly in the hands of consumers, who now had the strongest and most important voice in the conversation. Engagement was the word.
AUTHENTIC MARKETING ERA 2018-	To thrive and truly engage in today's elaborate environment, we need to continue to push marketing to its most evolved form yet – one of authenticity. The missing critical piece – moral purpose – holds the potential to propel companies by adding the values and ethical impact customers crave and demand.

Source: *Authentic Marketing* (Larry Weber).

2. MARKETERS: SUPERVILLAINS OR SUPERHEROES?

If you look back over the years, there's little doubt that some blame can be placed at the door of marketing for its contribution to unhealthy lifestyles, obesity, debt, low self-esteem, mental health, materialism and general over-consumption.

Creative thinking and the art of persuasive communication has led many people to buy many products that they neither need nor really want.

Put bluntly here in the book *Good is The New Cool, Market Like You Give A Damn* (Aziz + Jones):

> "Marketers have helped to create a culture of materialistic excess that has led to a cancer of overconsumption.
>
> And even today marketers are all too often guilty of 'greenwashing' or 'brandwashing' – marketing their brands and corporations as paragons of virtue while ignoring insidious practices and reprehensible behaviour behind the scenes."

So, many would agree that marketers need to take a certain degree of responsibility for causing some of our current environmental and societal issues. But there is a big difference between marketers simply trying to do the best they can with a bad brief (or no brief), as opposed to consciously manipulating the truth.

The net result is however that marketing helps companies sell more of their stuff (good or bad).

So are marketers forever condemned to be the Supervillains or can they adopt the role of the sustainability Superhero?

Marketers have the skills to educate and encourage ethical and sustainable behaviour – from the boardroom to the shopping trolley – clearly articulating the financial benefits of corporate sensitivity to people and the planet, plus championing the responsible use and disposal of products.

In order to do this, marketing needs to become the conscience of the business, not just be seen as a PR tool.

3. GREENWASHING WON'T WASH

> **WHITEWASH** (verb): *to make something bad seem acceptable by hiding the truth.*
>
> **GREENWASH** (verb): *to make people believe that your company is doing more to protect the environment than it really is.*

You don't have to be perfect, but you absolutely need to be honest when you consider promoting your ethical and sustainable credentials. False marketing claims will be exposed, and that all-important trust will be lost overnight.

GREENWASHING IS RIFE:

- 26% of companies have no proof to back up their claims
- 11% of labelling is vague
- 4% of green claims are irrelevant
- 1% even make claims to distract customers from deficiencies (such as 'organically grown tobacco')
- 1% are out-and-out lies

Source: *The Sustainable Business* (Jonathan T Scott)

Ethical marketing requires complete transparency. Be proud of your positive actions but also acknowledge and be honest about the areas that you need to work on. Then tell customers what you plan to do about it and when. Don't be afraid of outlining why it's not an easy, quick fix.

If there are suspicions over claims in your marketing, consider commissioning an independent source to audit and verify your claims. You may be surprised at the result.

4. TOO LITTLE, TOO TRIUMPHANT, TOO LATE?

It's not just greenwashing you have to watch out for. Many companies come unstuck in their marketing when they fail to understand the bigger picture.

This usually falls into the following categories: too little, too triumphant, too late.

So consider the following.

IS IT TOO LITTLE?

- Is this claim too insignificant in the grand scale of things?
- Do we run the risk of being ridiculed for this?
- Will this simply highlight bigger areas of the business that are currently unethical?

Example: Companies proudly reporting that they have removed plastic straws from the business, while simultaneously ignoring all other single use plastics being used throughout the organization.

IS IT TOO TRIUMPHANT?

- Is this an isolated claim that we are making an overly big fuss about?
- Could this solicit negative customer feedback because it feels somewhat incongruent in relation to other unethical parts of the business?

Example: Companies making a huge song and dance about one ethical activity such as charity giving, while continuing to adopt unethical and unsustainable practices elsewhere in the organization.

IS IT TOO LATE?

- Have all our competitors been doing this for ages?
- Does this simply highlight how late to the party we are?

Example: Companies reporting to care deeply about customers' data and requesting that they re-subscribe for special and unique offers and promotions, in the very month that GDPR (General Data Protection Regulation) becomes a legal requirement.

Be honest with this assessment and ruthlessly analyse possible marketing claims from a purely marketing perspective. They may be true, but will they be positively received?

5. CHECK, CLARIFY, CHALLENGE, CHANGE

It is natural for people to have an over-inflated view of their brands, products or services, but some professional cross-examination of claims and statements can flush out the dubious, the doubtful, and the delusional.

Here's a framework that can help anyone interrogate a claim. It encourages looking at it from a *legal* and a *moral* perspective, and:

- checking the facts,
- clarifying the details,
- challenging like a customer, and
- changing where necessary.

WHAT IS THE MARKETING CLAIM?

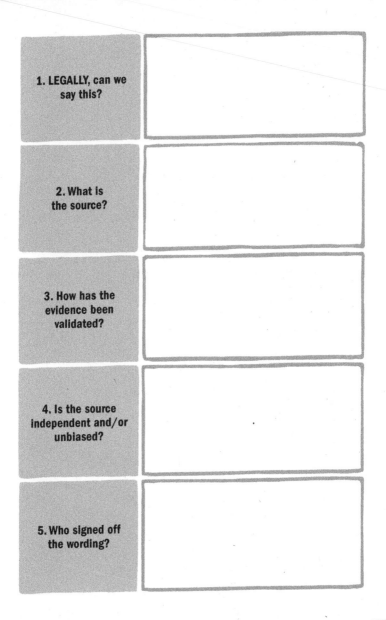

1. LEGALLY, can we say this?

2. What is the source?

3. How has the evidence been validated?

4. Is the source independent and/or unbiased?

5. Who signed off the wording?

6. MORALLY, should we say this?

7. What are we potentially overstating?

8. Is this only part of the story? What is not being mentioned?

9. What could customers be wary of?

10. Are they right to be wary? How can we address this?

What needs to be ....

CHECKED?

CLARIFIED?

CHALLENGED?

CHANGED?

6. BOGOF REINVENTED – BUY ONE, GIVE ONE FREE

One of the most tangible societal strategies a company can consider builds on the paying it forward approach (Part 3.8).

Once you have identified people who would benefit most from your product or service but are unable to afford it, you can develop a plan to incorporate an element of free distribution as part of your triple bottom line business plan.

For the ultimate in clear, powerful marketing messages, you can reinvent the old promotional tool of Buy One Get One Free to **Buy One GIVE One Free.**

This is now being successfully used by a number of innovative, thoughtful businesses:

TOMS SHOES
Toms Shoes improves lives through a programme they call One for One. For every product purchased they provide shoes, sight, water, safe birth and bullying prevention services to people in need.

MINDFUL CHEF

Mindful Chef, a healthy food recipe and delivery service, runs a programme called One Feeds Two. With every meal purchased, they donate a school meal to a child in poverty, which has amounted to over five million so far.

HEY GIRLS

Hey Girls tackles period poverty in the UK by giving a free box of sanitary towels to women and girls in need for every box purchased. This buy one give one approach gives girls the freedom to enjoy normal lives without having to miss school, ask friends for products or simply go without.

Not all organizations can commit to the full buy one, give one model. If this doesn't work for your business, consider instead a **Buy One, Give SOMETHING** approach.

Another initiative that you may already be aware of is Pledge 1% – pioneered by SalesForce.org. Here companies pledge to annually give 1% of equity, 1% of profits, 1% of product and/or 1% of employee time to worthy causes.

So consider to whom you could give your product (time and/or profit) and how it could become part of your marketing story.

7. NAVIGATING THE COMPETITION

The market mapping tool is a highly effective and very flexible way to establish clarity and strategic authority when looking at any market.

In this instance, it can be used to monitor your ethical progress and integrity against your competition. This is a fast-moving area, so this exercise needs to be done regularly to ensure your ethical authority is justified – to check that your competitors are not outdoing your achievements and therefore rendering your marketing claims weak or untrue.

For this 'ethical' exercise, we will use a vertical axis on Profitability against a horizontal axis of Ethical Credentials. Place your company plus your competitors on the grid. Use the results to identify where you currently sit within your marketplace against where you would like to be.

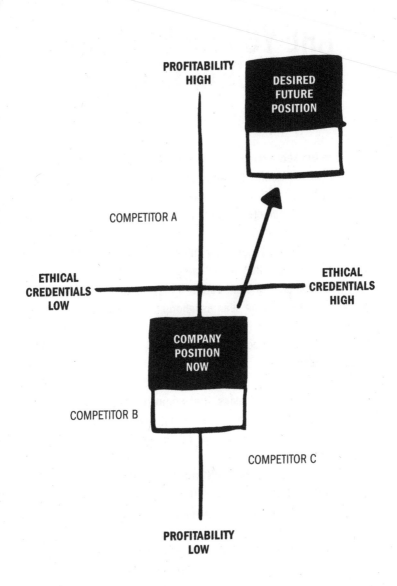

PROFITABILITY
HIGH

DESIRED
FUTURE
POSITION

COMPETITOR A

ETHICAL
CREDENTIALS
LOW

ETHICAL
CREDENTIALS
HIGH

COMPANY
POSITION
NOW

COMPETITOR B

COMPETITOR C

PROFITABILITY
LOW

8. ARE YOU AN ETHICAL GAME CHANGER?

The Three Buckets exercise was introduced by Adam Morgan in his book *The Pirate Inside*. It is an extremely helpful way to categorize ideas or projects and work out how effective they are likely to be and also how genuinely 'unique' they are.

In the case of ethical marketing initiatives, it's important that you have the right mix. If they are all fairly basic, you will struggle to stand out against your competitors. If they are all overly innovative, you run the risk of being seen as ignoring the obvious.

The exercise is to place ideas and initiatives in one of the three buckets.

On the left is **Brilliant Basics**. These represent 'excellence as standard'. You or your company should really be doing these well as a matter of course, just like your competitors.

In the middle is **Compelling Difference**. These should be 'significantly better than normal'. These are demonstrably better than your competitors, but not genuinely remarkable.

On the right is **Changing the Game**. These are 'truly extraordinary'. They are utterly distinctive in the market and genuinely remarkable.

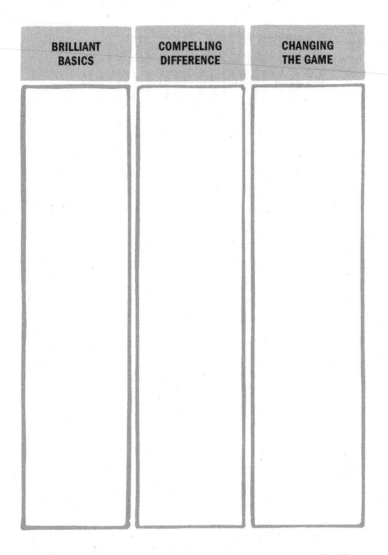

BRILLIANT BASICS	COMPELLING DIFFERENCE	CHANGING THE GAME

Ideally, everything on the left should be underway or completed.
If there is nothing in the middle or right, you need better initiatives.

9. MINIMUM EFFORT, MAXIMUM RETURN

Once you have your comprehensive list of ethical and sustainable initiatives, it's important to prioritize these and balance business impact with the effort or resources required. It is better to complete a few really important initiatives than to start many and finish few.

Here's a neat framework adapted from the book *Conscious Capitalism Field Guide* (Sisodia, Henry, Eckschmidt), which allows you to compare the estimated resources required (effort) against the impact on the business – whether that's customer excitement, employee engagement, environmental protection or financial reward (return).

Resources are relative to the size of your organization. What might take three or four people would be a high resource in a start-up, but easy for a large organization.

Using this matrix will help you identify four types of initiative:

TOP LEFT: High return, low effort initiatives = do them now
TOP RIGHT: High return, high effort initiatives = plan them now
BOTTOM LEFT: Low effort, low return initiatives = think on
BOTTOM RIGHT: High effort, low return initiatives = ignore

Gather your team together and spend as long as the business requires filling in the matrix. Then draw up an action plan based on the outcome.

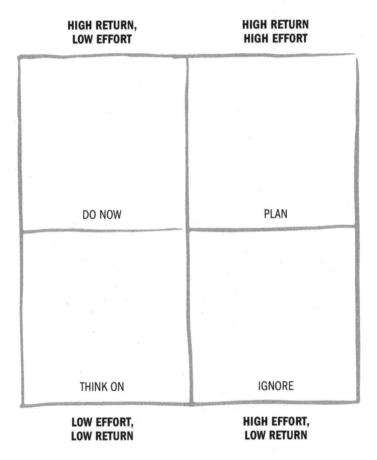

HIGH RETURN, LOW EFFORT	HIGH RETURN HIGH EFFORT
DO NOW	PLAN
THINK ON	IGNORE
LOW EFFORT, LOW RETURN	HIGH EFFORT, LOW RETURN

10. STORYDOING AND DATATELLING

Larry Weber's *Authentic Marketing* talks of storydoing and datatelling. As the author says, this may sound like marketing speak, but it's really about moving your organization from telling stories to actually being an active part of them. This is all about showing what your company is *doing* to solve a problem to make the world a better place.

As has been highlighted throughout this book, it is important to outline measurable objectives that your company can realistically accomplish in a certain time period – then track and measure them as you make progress. Quantifiable data is important to validate this progress and should be included in the narrative. It can be used to create simple and powerful visuals, charts, graphs and marketing claims.

Here are some techniques for creating compelling, ongoing stories that bring your brand's ethical journey to life.

TELL IT VISUALLY	Without a doubt, visual is the best format today. Repurpose stories across multiple visual media for maximum impact.
BE SELECTIVE WITH WORDS	Use words that are vibrant, descriptive, evoke emotions, ignite the senses and draw readers in.
HIGHLIGHT HUMILITY	Bring forth the people in your stories. Share their voices (including employees, customers and suppliers).
LET CREATIVITY SHINE	Make the best use of the technical tools now readily available and tell stories with creativity.
KEEP IT REAL	People will sniff out even the slightest hint of manipulation or marketing speak – so keep it honest and genuine, with a little dose of humility (and no hubris).
ENSURE IT'S ALWAYS ON	Your company's ethical journey will have a beginning and many chapters but should not have an end. It should be living, breathing and evolving.

MARKETING RECAP

1. Understand the characteristics of the authentic marketing era
2. Become a sustainability superhero
3. Audit and remove any examples of greenwashing
4. Screen all marketing claims that may be too little, too late, or too triumphant
5. Check, Clarify, Challenge, and Change marketing claims where necessary
6. Work out who you could give your product to for free, and how it would fit into your marketing story
7. Keep track of your claims in relation to those of your competition and how they are changing
8. Conduct a three buckets exercise
9. Complete the minimal effort, maximum return grid
10. Use storydoing and datatelling to add greater marketing integrity

NOTES

A-Z OF COMMONLY USED TERMS

All subjects have their jargon and acronyms. These plain English definitions should help you navigate the topic with confidence.

Alt-proteins: *Alternative proteins, or meat alternatives, are plant-based or food-technology ('clean meat') alternatives to animal protein.*

Anthropocene: *Current geological age, viewed as the period in which human activity has been the dominant influence on climate and the environment.*

Biodegradable: *Capable of being decomposed by bacteria or other living organisms and thereby avoiding pollution.*

Biodiversity: *The variety of life on Earth, including all plant and animal species.*

Biomass: *Plant or animal material used for energy production, or in industrial processes as raw substance for various products. Types include purposely-grown energy crops, wood or forest residues, waste from food crops, horticulture, food processing, animal farming, or human waste from sewage plants.*

Biomimicry: *Emulating the models, systems, and elements of nature to solve complex human problems.*

Blockchain: *A digital record of transactions. The name comes from its structure, in which individual records called blocks are linked together in a single list, called a chain.*

Carbon capture and storage (CCS): *The process of capturing and storing carbon dioxide before it is released into the atmosphere.*

Carbon credit: *A permit which allows a country or organization to produce a certain amount of carbon emissions and which can be traded if the full allowance is not used.*

Carbon dioxide: *A naturally occurring gas in Earth's atmosphere. It is the main greenhouse gas released by human activities such as burning fossil fuels and biomass, industrial processes, and land-use change.*

Carbon footprint: *The amount of carbon dioxide released into the atmosphere as a result of the activities of a particular individual, organization, or community.*

Carbon offsetting: *A carbon offset is a reduction in emissions of carbon dioxide or other greenhouse gases made to compensate for emissions made elsewhere. Offsets are measured in tonnes of carbon dioxide equivalent.*

Carbon neutrality: *Carbon neutrality refers to achieving net zero carbon dioxide emissions by balancing them with removal elsewhere or eliminating them altogether.*

Carbon tax: *A carbon tax is a tax levied on the carbon content of fuels, in sectors like transport and energy. Carbon taxes aim to reduce carbon dioxide emissions by increasing the price of fossil fuels and decreasing the demand for them. They are a form of carbon pricing.*

Circular economy: *A circular economy is based on the principles of designing out waste and pollution, keeping products and materials in use, and regenerating natural systems.*

Climate change: *A significant change in climate persisting over an extended period of time, typically for a number of decades or more.*

Climate crisis: *A headline descriptor for the threat of dangerous and irreversible changes to the world's climate.*

Climate positive: *Climate positive describes an activity that goes beyond achieving net zero carbon emissions to creating an environmental benefit by removing additional carbon dioxide from the atmosphere.*

Closed loop: *A system that does not accept inputs from, or create outputs to, another system.*

Conscious consumerism: *Increased consumer awareness of the impact of their purchase decisions on the environment and society.*

COP: *A Conference Of Parties is the governing body of an international convention – in this context to discuss global climate change.*

Cradle to cradle: *A sustainable business strategy that mimics the regenerative cycle of nature in which waste is reused. Building on the cradle to grave approach of decreasing waste, cradle to cradle goes a step further and attempts to eliminate waste altogether.*

CSR: *Corporate Social Responsibility is a management concept in which companies integrate social and environmental concerns into their business operations and interactions with suppliers and customers.*

Doughnut economics: *A visual framework for sustainable development – shaped like a doughnut – combining the concept of planetary boundaries with the complementary concept of social boundaries.*

Downstream emissions: *Emissions that occur in the life cycle of a material/ product after the sale by the producer (including distribution and storage, use of the product and end-of-life).*

Earth overshoot day: *This marks the date each year when humanity has exhausted nature's budget for the year, as tracked by: footprintnetwork.org.*

Ecosystem: *A natural system consisting of all living organisms (plants, animals, and microorganisms) in a specific area functioning together.*

Environmental footprint: *The effect that a person, company, or activity has on the environment - for example, the amount of natural resources used and the amount of harmful greenhouse gases (GHGs) produced.*

ESG: *Environmental, Social, and Corporate Governance refers to the three central factors in measuring the sustainability and societal impact of financial investment in a company or business venture.*

Ethical: *Relating to beliefs about what is morally right and wrong.*

Fairtrade: *Fairtrade refers to producers in developing countries being paid a fair price for their work by companies in developed countries. The price paid provides enough for producers to afford essentials such as food, education and healthcare.*

Fossil fuels: *Fossil fuels are made from decomposing plants and animals. They are found in the Earth's crust and contain carbon and hydrogen, which can be burned for energy. Examples include coal, oil, and natural gas.*

Frugal innovation: *Frugal innovation or frugal engineering is the process of reducing the complexity and cost of goods and their production. It usually refers to removing nonessential features from goods such as cars or mobile phones often to sell them in developing countries.*

Global warming: *The gradual increase in Earth's average atmospheric and ocean temperatures.*

Good Life Goals: *The Good Life Goals (created by the World Business Council for Sustainable Development) are 17 suggestions that explain how individuals can change their personal behaviour to help achieve the equivalent Sustainable Development Goals. (see Sustainable Development Goals)*

Great acceleration: *A term referring to the world's unprecedented growth since around the 1950s and, as a result, the unprecedented deterioration of the natural resources needed to fuel this growth.*

Green recovery: *Packages of environmental, regulatory and fiscal reforms to recover prosperity in a responsible way after the COVID-19 pandemic.*

Greenhouse gases (GHGs): *Atmospheric gases of human or natural origin that absorb and emit heat. This results in heat being trapped in the climate system. The main greenhouse gases in the atmosphere include carbon dioxide, nitrous oxide and methane.*

Green growth: *A path of economic growth that uses resources in a sustainable way (unlike traditional economic growth that typically does not account for environmental damage).*

Greenwashing: *To make people believe that your company is doing more to protect the environment than it really is.*

Human capital: *Value derived from employees: physical presence, knowledge, skills, abilities, intellectual capacity, spirituality, empathy, and passion.*

Impact investing: *Investments made with the intention of generating positive, measurable social and environmental impact as well as a financial return.*

Inertia principle: *This is a guiding principle of the circular economy, as introduced by Walter Stahel. "Do not repair what is not broken, do not remanufacture something that can be repaired, do not recycle a product that can be remanufactured. Replace or treat only the smallest possible part in order to maintain the existing economic value".*

LGBTQ: *Acronym for lesbian, gay, bisexual, transgender and queer or questioning - terms are used to describe a person's sexual orientation or gender identity.*

Living wage: *A wage that is high enough to maintain a normal standard of living in the relevant country.*

Linear economy: *A linear economy traditionally follows the "take-make-use-waste" plan. Raw materials are collected and transformed into products that are used until they are discarded as waste.*

Manufactured capital: *Infrastructure and tangible goods that an organisation owns (or leases) to produce its outputs.*

Moral: *Relating to the standards of good or bad behaviour, fairness, honesty, etc. that each person believes in, rather than to laws.*

Natural capital: *The world's stocks of natural assets, which include geology, soil, air, water and all living things. From this humans get: food, drinking water, plants (for medicine, fuel, building materials), natural flood defences, carbon storage (peatlands, etc), and pollination of crops from insects.*

Natural capitalism: *A global economy in which business and environmental interests overlap, recognizing the interdependencies that exist between the production and use of human-made capital and flows of natural capital.*

Nature-based solutions: *The use of nature to jointly tackle social and environmental issues, such as climate change, food and water security, pollution and disaster risk. For example, reforestation to act as a natural carbon capture and storage (CSS) facility.*

Net zero: *A state in which the activities of a company result in no net impact on climate from greenhouse gas emissions. This is achieved by reducing emissions to zero or counterbalancing their effect with an appropriate amount of carbon removal elsewhere in the business.*

Organic: *Relating to or derived from living matter.*

Planetary boundaries: *Set of nine parameters within which humanity can develop and thrive for generations to come, so long as they are not exceeded.*

Recycling: *The action or process of converting waste into reusable material.*

Remanufacturing: *To manufacture into a new product.*

Repurposing: *Finding a new use for an idea, product, or building.*

Rewild: *Restore an area of land to its natural state, either through the reintroduction of species that have been driven out or exterminated, or by returning the land to natural, usually non-agricultural use.*

Science based targets initiative (SBTI): *The Science Based Targets initiative champions science-based target setting to boost companies' competitive advantage in the transition to the low-carbon economy. It is a collaboration between Carbon Disclosure Project (CDP), the United Nations Global Compact (UNGC), World Resources Institute (WRI), the*

World Wide Fund for Nature (WWF), and one of the We Mean Business Coalition commitments.

Sustainable: *Able to continue over a period of time. In relation to the environment, causing little or no damage to the environment and therefore able to continue for a long time.*

Sustainable Development Goals (SDGs): *The 17 goals adopted by all United Nations Member States in 2015 as a universal call to action to end poverty, protect the planet and ensure that all people enjoy peace and prosperity by 2030. (see Good Life Goals)*

Stakeholder: *In a corporation, a stakeholder is a member of groups without whose support the organization would cease to exist, as defined in the first use of the word in a 1963 internal memorandum at the Stanford Research Institute.*

Tipping point: *The critical point in a situation, process, or system beyond which a significant and often unstoppable effect or change takes place.*

Upcycling: *Upcycling, also known as creative reuse, is the process of transforming by-products, waste materials, or unwanted products into new materials or products perceived to be of greater quality – often through artistic or environmental value.*

Upstream emissions: *Emissions that occur in the life cycle of a material/ product up to the point of sale by the producer.*

RESOURCES AND FURTHER READING

The body of literature on ethical and sustainable business practice is growing steadily. At the time of writing, I have read the main titles easily available. One-page summaries can be found at: ethicalbusinessblog.com. Do check back regularly as this library will continue to be updated after the publication of this book.

50 Ways To Help The Planet, Sian Berry (Kyle Books, 2018)

A Safe and Just Space for Humanity, Kate Raworth (Oxfam Discussion Document, 2012)

Authentic Marketing, Larry Weber (John Wiley, 2019)

All In, David Grayson, Chris Coulter & Mark Lee (Routledge 2018)

Better, John Grant (Unbound, 2018)

Brand Manners, Hamish Pringle & William Gordon (Wiley, 2003)

Business Ethics, Crane, Matten, Glozer, Spence (Oxford University Press, 2016)

Clever, Rob Goffee & Gareth R Jones (Harvard Business Review Press, 2009)

Compassion Inc, Gaurav Sinha (Ebury Press, 2018)

Conscious Capitalism Field Guide, Raj Sisodia, Timothy Henry & Thomas Eckschmidt (Harvard Business Review Press, 2018)

Conscious Leadership, Mackey, McIntosh, Cripps (Portfolio Penguin, 2020)

Diversify, June Sarpong (HQ, 2017)

Doughnut Economics, Kate Raworth (Random House, 2017)

Drive, Daniel Pink (Canongate, 2011)

Engaging for success: enhancing performance through employee engagement, Macleod Report, 2012

Ethical Marketing and the New Consumer, Chris Arnold (John Wiley, 2009)

False Alarm, Bjorn Lomborg (Basic, 2020)

Frugal Innovation, Radjou & Prabhu (Profile Books, 2016)

Good Is The New Cool, Aziz & Jones (Regan Arts, 2016)

Green Swans, John Elkington (Fast Company Press, 2020)

Greener Marketing, John Grant (Wiley, 2020)

How Bad Are Bananas?, Mike Berners-Lee (Profile, 2020)

Humane Capital, Vlatka Hlupic (Bloomsbury, 2019)

Millennial Employee Engagement Study, Cone Communications, 2016

Natural Capital, Dieter Helm (Yale University Press 2015)

No Bullshit Leadership, Chris Hirst (Profile Books, 2019)

No One Is Too Small To Make A Difference, Greta Thunberg (Penguin, 2019)

Our Final Warning, Mark Lynas (4th Estate, 2020)

Sustainable Business: A One Planet Approach, Sally Jeanrenaud, Jean-Paul Jeanrenaud & Jonathan Gosling (John Wiley, 2016)

The Ethical Capitalist, Julian Richer (Random House, 2018)

The Ethical Leader, Morgen Witzel (Bloomsbury, 2018)

The Five Dysfunctions of a Team, Patrick Lencioni (John Wiley, 2002)

The Future We Choose, Figueres & Rivett-Carnac (Manilla Press, 2020)

The Infinite Game, Simon Sinek (Penguin, 2019)

The Joyful Environmentalist, Isabel Losada (Watkins, 2020)

The Joy of Work, Bruce Daisley (Random House, 2019)

The New Brand Spirit, Christian Conrad & Marjorie Ellis Thompson
(Gower Publishing, 2013)

The New Rules of Green Marketing, Jacquelyn Ottman (Greenleaf, 2010)

The Pirate Inside, Adam Morgan (John Wiley, 2004)

There is no Planet B, Mike Berners-Lee (Cambridge University Press, 2019)

The Sales Person's Secret Code, Ian Mills, Mark Ridley, Ben Laker & Tim
Chapman (LID, 2017)

The Sustainable Business, Jonathan T Scott (Greenleaf, 2013)

The Uninhabitable Earth, David Wallace-Wells (Allen Lane, 2019)

We Are The Weather, Jonathan Safran Foer (Penguin, 2019)

WEconomy, Craig Kielburger, Holly Branson & Marc Kielburger (John Wiley, 2018)

Who Cares Wins, David Jones (Pearson, 2012)

Why Should Anyone Work Here?, Rob Goffee & Gareth Jones
(Harvard Business Review Press, 2015)

BCorporation.net /CarbonTrust.com / Defra.gov.uk /

Ellenmacarthurfoundation.org / Ethicalconsumer.org /

ExponentialRoadmap.org / GhgProtocol.org /Goodbusinesscharter.com /

HeyGirls.co.uk / Interface.com / Mindfulchef.com / Salesforce.org /

TheSRA.org / Toms.co.uk / UN.org/sustainabledevelopment / WBCSD.org

ACKNOWLEDGMENTS

Many thanks for the wise comments and amazing endorsements from Mark Earls, Jon Khoo, Giles Gibbons, Peter Hancock, Stephan Loerke, Dr Sally Marlow, Fergus Boyd, Steven Day, Paul Edwards, Marjorie Ellis Thompson, Chris Hirst, Richard Morris, Hamish Pringle, Mark Smith, Kaye Taylor, Ceri Tinley and Kate Thompson.

Thanks also for the kind words of support from Andrew White (Triggerfish PR), Cameron Wilson (EcoAct) and Jane Pendlebury (HOSPA). Plus a big shout out to Sara Marshall for all her loveliness and constant encouragement.

To my amazing and talented stepdaughters, Rosie and Shaunagh: I cannot thank you enough for your enthusiasm, insights and invaluable contributions to this book.

And finally, my love and thanks go to my husband Kevin, for being just all round bloody marvellous.

The world is a better place with you people in it.

ABOUT THE AUTHOR

SARAH DUNCAN is a sustainable business development and ethical marketing consultant and trainer. She has been in business for over 30 years – starting with luxury hotels, then moving through private club and spa development in Asia, to setting up her own consultancy, Sleeping Lion, in 2005.

She has watched with interest as sustainability has forced its way onto the business agenda, driven collectively by more ethically conscious employees and customers. She has recently completed a course with Cambridge University Institute of Sustainability Leadership in Business Sustainability Management.

She now helps businesses navigate their way through the world of business ethics and sustainability with advice, support and bespoke workshops.

Contact the author for consultancy, training or speaking opportunities:

sarah@sleepinglion.co.uk
@sleepinglion888
ethicalbusinessblog.com
sleepingliononline.com

BY THE SAME AUTHOR

£9.99/$14.95
978-1-911687-80-1